Common Spaces Between Us

Common Spaces Between Us

Nurturing the Good in the Midst of Difference

Melynne Rust

WIPF & STOCK · Eugene, Oregon

COMMON SPACES BETWEEN US
Nurturing the Good in the Midst of Difference

Wipf & Stock
An Imprint of Wipf and Stock Publishers
199 W. 8th Ave., Suite 3
Eugene, OR 97401

www.wipfandstock.com

PAPERBACK ISBN: 978-1-7252-5110-6
HARDCOVER ISBN: 978-1-7252-5111-3
EBOOK ISBN: 978-1-7252-5112-0

Manufactured in the U.S.A.   DECEMBER 5, 2019

All Scripture quotations are from New Revised Standard Version Bible,
copyright © 1989 National Council of the Churches of Christ in the United
States of America. Used by permission.

Portions of this book previously appeared in different form on collegevil-
leinstitute.org, quantumtheology.blogspot.com, amypeterson.net, and in
The Avion.

This is a work of nonfiction based upon the author's experiences as a college chaplain. To protect the privacy of the individuals described, most
names and certain identifying details have been changed. In addition,
some chronology has been modified.

For my children,
Wilson, Meredith, and April,
who taught me how to nurture the good in college students.

And for the college students
who taught me how to nurture the good in my children
through their college years.

Awaken my senses this day
to the goodness that still stems from Eden.
Awaken my senses
to the goodness that can still spring forth
in me and in all that has life.
—J PHILIP NEWELL, *CELTIC BENEDICTION*

Contents

Preface

IN AMERICAN CULTURE TODAY, where the loudest chant throughout our polarized society seems to be "us versus them," it can be exhausting to try and connect with others in the midst of our deep differences. It can be especially wearisome when we come up against people who are difficult or demanding or who diminish us for one reason or another. We can end up feeling discouraged, even defeated, in our attempts to authentically connect with others who we feel are so different from us. And then, on top of all this, we may also discover along the way that we have come up against our own inner dilemmas. At least, this has been what has happened with me.

My personal chant is that I believe in the dignity and equality of all human beings. And I am committed to living out these values I say I believe, yet sometimes I find I betray myself in subtle ways—maybe by my fear or my silence or my lack of awareness. And if I am honest with myself—if I pay attention to the wisdom of my inner voice—I sometimes find, despite my best intentions and commitment to equality, that I might harbor some judgments about certain groups of people who look or speak or believe differently from me, or particular kinds of people who behave differently than me, or maybe specific individuals who I feel seek to denigrate me.

This is some of what I stumbled upon when I went to work as a chaplain on an incredibly diverse college campus. Everywhere I turned I encountered people who looked, believed, and behaved differently than me. And much to my surprise and chagrin, I found myself struggling at times to authentically connect with them amid cultural and religious diversity, sexual identity differences, mental illness stigmas, domestic violence, philosophical ideologies, and generational and behavioral dynamics.

For example, I butted heads with students who shared my religion but not my beliefs. I resisted reaching out to a student who was abusing his girlfriend. I stubbornly wondered why the Muslim students thought they needed bidets in the chapel bathrooms.

Sometimes it was my fear of the unknown or fear of the stranger or fear of difference in and of itself. Sometimes it was fear of what others might think of me that kept me from being true to my values. Other times it was because I had not realized I was not valuing myself the way I said (and believed) I wanted to value others. There were times I was complicit in dehumanizing others by remaining silent when I could have spoken up. And then there were times I said something judgmental when, in retrospect, it would have behooved me to remain quiet.

At some point, though, I became cognizant to the reality that, as a chaplain, I had the unique privilege of being drawn into the inner spaces of my students' lives. And I noticed it was often there in those spaces that I encountered the capacity to fully see, hear, and value them in the midst of our differences. It was often in those common spaces between us that we experienced the potential to recognize, honor, and nurture the good in one another.

A confession from a Catholic student opened my eyes to what it means to make room for students who share my religion but not my beliefs. A conversation with the violent boyfriend reminded me of our shared humanity. And standing in a bathroom stall with the Muslim students as they advocated for their bidets helped me recognize the gifts others have to offer.

My particular encounters provided insight into more universal questions I had been asking myself: In the midst of so much difference, how can any of us live out the values we claim about the dignity and equality of all human beings? How can we create connection with others when deep in our hearts we might harbor shadows of judgment or fear? What would help us to show up in those common spaces between us and really see and hear and value one another?

Through my experiences I became more aware of the shadows that get in the way of authentic connection across difference, and I discovered ways to illuminate those shadows and cultivate the capacity to see beyond them. Sometimes it means acknowledging our fears and making room for others by creating a safe space. Sometimes it means remembering we are all human beings, and spiritual beings too. Sometimes it is about paying attention to the worthiness of our own inner voice. Other times it is about suspending judgment and showing kindness, both with others and with ourselves. And it is about recognizing the gifts others have to offer, especially when we are inclined to think we are the ones bringing the gifts.

All these ways, or "practices of nurture" (as I call them), have the potential to remind us who we want to be and prompt us to embody the values we embrace. They teach us how, in the midst of our polarized society—our polarized communities and churches and schools and families and friendships—we can intentionally choose to recognize, honor, and nurture the good in one another and thereby foster connection.

Embedded in story, these practices of nurture show us how to live out a narrative that claims—like the New Zealand prime minister claimed after the recent massacre of Muslim citizens in her country—"they are us."[1] And we are them.

1. For more information see "Jacinda Ardern," https://www.theguardian.com/world/2019/mar/15/one-of-new-zealands-darkest-days-jacinda-ardern-responds-to-christchurch-shooting.

Acknowledgments

THE SEED FOR THIS book was planted at a summer writing workshop at Collegeville Institute. After the workshop participants had provided feedback on my twenty-page essay about my days as a college chaplain, Lauren Winner, the workshop facilitator, suggested that my essay could be the makings of a book. I had felt like this long(ish) essay had exhausted my capabilities as a writer; and so, at the time, the idea of writing an entire book felt like a daunting declaration. And yet, the little seed Lauren planted began to take hold in my heart, and before long I found myself pondering the possibilities. Thank you, Lauren, for stirring and inspiring this latent desire within me, and for modeling so effortlessly how to write about spiritual things "without preaching or falling into dogma." Also, thank you to the participants of that workshop who, each in your own way, contributed to my understanding of what it means to write creatively. And to the people of Collegeville Institute, thank you for your investment of time and resources in cultivating new writers and supporting our work.

For the team at Wipf and Stock Publishers, thank you for your commitment to writing that "honors the imagination, intellect, and heart"; and thank you for inviting this book to find a home in the hands of those who desire to read books that honor the imagination, intellect, and heart.

For Christianne Squires, founder of Bookwifery, Inc., and my editor and spiritual guide, you have been a godsend. You in all your diverse giftedness were exactly what I needed to move forward with this work. Thank you for believing this book could be more than I imagined it to be. You have nurtured, encouraged, and challenged me to face my fears as you have companioned me through this writing adventure. And for the Bookwifery Collective community of writers, you all have become the balm for my writer's soul. Thank you for your solidarity, your wisdom, and your generous spirits.

For Missy Hart, who has read every word of every draft I have written, and who I sometimes think knows me better than I know myself, thank you for abiding with me; and thank you for graciously reminding me who I am, especially when I am inclined to let my words tell a different story. I could not have done this without you patiently loving me through it.

For Sherry McElveen, thank you for your faithful presence on Wednesday mornings, in listening to my woes and celebrating my highs throughout this endeavor. You have been a sanctuary. And for my bookclub cohorts, thank you for surrounding me with your circle of love and for being some of my staunchest cheerleaders.

For the students, staff, and faculty who I have had the privilege to work with, it is in your company that I learned to be a chaplain. Thank you for welcoming me into your campus community and into the common spaces between us. It is my sincerest hope that this book honors you.

And for my children, Wilson, Meredith, and April, you are the breath of my being. Mothering the three of you through your college years made me a more compassionate chaplain. And being a college chaplain during your college years made me a wiser and gentler mother. I am grateful for the serendipitous opportunity to do both simultaneously. This book is for you. May you always nurture the good in one another.

CHAPTER I

Eyes of the Cadets

Practice of Nurture: Acknowledge Your Fears

I HAD JUST STEPPED out of the shower on a rainy Tuesday morning in mid-September when my cell phone rang. I had interviewed for a position at a local university twice the week before and had been told they would make a decision over the weekend. As Monday slipped away, so had my hope. But then, at eight o'clock that Tuesday morning, the human resources director was on the phone, offering me the job.

I wrapped a towel around myself, cradling the phone between my ear and shoulder, and nervously told her I accepted. The words were barely out of my mouth, however, when she began to apologize. In all her years in human resources, she said, she had never had to make this request, but the Dean of Students Office had wanted her to inquire if I could start working that very day.

"*Today?*" I asked, my voice rising several octaves as my towel began to slip. Before even thinking, almost indignant, I started to ramble: "I still have my current job, you know. I have to resign from that position, give them several weeks at least, maybe more, I don't know. I have meetings and projects and loose ends to tie up. There's just no way I can start today."

I took a breath and somehow had the presence of mind to wonder aloud, "Why would the Dean of Students Office want me to start today?"

There was a long pause, and then a clearing of her throat. When finally she spoke, her words came out squeaky and in spurts, as if with each little pause she was sipping up courage to speak.

"We had a student who died last night . . . collapsed while running with the ROTC group . . . could not be revived . . . freshman . . . eighteen years old. His name was Jonathan."

And then, all at once, she said, "The Dean of Students Office wants to know if there's any way you could meet with them this afternoon to help them work through this crisis."

Oh. Oh dear.

My planned day evaporated in my mind, and I wondered how I would explain this to my current boss while also trying to remember my girls' afterschool activities. *Was there a volleyball game today or just practice? Would April get a ride with Meredith, or would I need to pick her up?*

"Of course," I responded. "Of course I can start today. Tell them I'll come by this afternoon."

Thus began my tenure as a college chaplain. Before another Tuesday came around, before I even had a nameplate on my new office door, I would have presided at my first memorial service for my first deceased student.

❧

The job posting had appeared on the college website the day before we took our son, Wilson, up to Auburn to start his freshman year, about a month before I was invited to interview. I was intrigued by the idea of working as a college chaplain. Although I'd never worked with college students, I figured they couldn't be that much different from my own three kids, who were eighteen, sixteen, and fourteen years old at the time. I applied for the position before I went to bed that night.

The next day was a typical sultry August morning in Florida, which only exaggerated the emotions that hovered in the air like the humidity. The entire family—me; my husband, Jay; and Wilson, Meredith, and April—squeezed into our minivan with the meager few items Wilson thought he needed for a year away at school (there had been arguments about this), and we began the seven-hour trek to Auburn University in Alabama.

For the most part, we kept quiet in the car, each of us into our own thoughts. I couldn't stop thinking about the day I walked Wilson to his classroom on his first day of kindergarten. Back then it was hard for me to imagine our days not following the same rhythm. Now I couldn't fathom what it would be like without him living in the same home or the same state or even the same time zone as me.

I wondered what he was thinking about. Was he thinking he would miss us? Or was he thinking that he couldn't wait to begin his new life, untethered from all of us—the same way I had been thinking when my parents drove me to college all those years ago?

I tried not to cry in front of him. I wanted to be excited for him. I *was* excited for him, I told myself. That is, until we helped him unpack his things in his new dorm room and I came upon a small brown paper lunch bag, wrinkled and stuffed in the side pocket of his duffel. Thinking it must be remnants from a long-ago lunch but wanting to make sure I didn't toss any reusable containers, I unfolded the bag and peered in.

Oh, my.

I felt my cheeks go hot.

This was no leftover lunch bag. Inside there must have been at least fifty—maybe sixty—little individual packages of condoms.

I looked up, and there was Wilson, flushed as well, staring at me from across the room. Our eyes locked for what felt like forever but couldn't possibly have been more than a few awkward seconds. Jay and the girls were oblivious, distracted by other tasks.

Wilson crossed the room and was by my side before I could blink.

"It's not what you think," he whispered, looking over his shoulder to make sure he hadn't attracted the attention of his dad or sisters. "The guys back home gave them to me as a joke. I mean, it's not like I'm going to use all those."

I wanted to say, *Okay, then, I'll just take them back home with me, since it's just a joke.* But his use of the word "all" brought me up short. That word indicated he probably planned to use at least *some* of them.

I realized then that the condoms themselves weren't the joke; it was the *number* of condoms that was the joke.

Okay. I get it.

But I didn't like it. The condoms reminded me of the stark reality that my son would be on his own, making decisions without my input or guidance or supervision. It made me afraid for him.

I folded up the bag and put it back in the side pocket of his duffle. Then I whispered, "Please be safe. Make good choices. And remember who you are."

For me, those words were not just about the condoms. They were what I wanted him to remember every time he encountered the freedom to make any choice he wanted to make. I wanted him to remember he was not alone in his decision-making, that he was still connected to a family who loved him and wanted the best for him.

He gave me a sheepish look and a one-armed side hug and whispered, "I will, Mom. I will."

It was not lost on me, the parallels between the deceased student, Jonathan, and Wilson. Jonathan, like Wilson, had matriculated to college in another state and another time zone a few short weeks ago. Jonathan, like Wilson, was only eighteen. Jonathan, like Wilson, was a healthy and vibrant young man. Like Wilson, he had his whole life in front of him.

Since Wilson had been gone, I had worried about so many things. I worried he wouldn't eat well and wouldn't get enough sleep. I worried he might sleep too much and not wake up in time for class. I worried about him making friends—but then, when he pledged a fraternity, I worried about him having too many friends. I worried about the hazing and the parties and the sex. *Was he using the condoms?*

Had Jonathan's mother worried about these things too?

I'd worried about these things, but it hadn't occurred to me to worry about death. How had I missed the most obvious worry? When I said my prayers, my liturgy of worries, my fears for my son, how had I neglected to mention death, the deepest fear a mother has?

I had let it lay unexamined, buried deep in the pile of fears that get sifted through.

Had Jonathan's mother neglected to worry about death too? Had she not allowed herself access to that fear until she received the phone call that ripped it right out of her womb and hurled it into her heart?

᷍

Because Jonathan had been enrolled in Reserve Officer Training Corps, the program for college students who want to enter the military as officers when they graduate, the ROTC Department requested a military-style memorial service for him. Esther, the long-reigning, no-nonsense administrative coordinator for the Chaplain's Office, sat me down and showed me the program from another ROTC service done a few years back. It was filled with the names of all kinds of official people, from the colonel to the college president to the dean of students—and then, near the bottom, the chaplain. I suggested to Esther that if all these other people would be speaking, perhaps I didn't need to. What would I have to say that wouldn't already have been said?

Esther looked at me like she was sorry I had been hired, then replied, "Of course you need to speak. You're the chaplain. All these other people have their parts, but you are the only one who will provide the spiritual solace we all need."

I will?

Esther assumed I had never done a military-style funeral before, and this much was true. What she didn't know, and what I didn't tell her, was that I had never done *any* kind of funeral before. I had no idea what I was doing, and my fear was causing me to forget who I was, to forget that I was the one who was called to offer comfort and peace and hope. Esther's words brought me back to myself.

I didn't know what I was going to say at Jonathan's service, but I knew what I wouldn't say. I wouldn't say, "This happened for a reason." Or, "He's in a better place." Or, "God needed another angel in heaven." I would not say, "This was God's will." I was convinced God did not cause Jonathan's death, nor did God have some master plan that could only be accomplished if Jonathan was no longer around. I thought of the saying attributed to King Solomon: "God did not make death, and he does not delight in the death of the living."[1] I also thought of all the ways Jesus worked to bring healing and wholeness, to bring life instead of death, to the people who encountered him. If he was the ultimate revelation of God, then his actions revealed that God did not orchestrate our deaths.

Underneath the easy clichés and the pointing to God were deep questions of meaning, of trying to make sense out of something that didn't make any sense. Eighteen-year-olds were not supposed to collapse and die. College students were not supposed to attend funerals for their friends. Mothers were not supposed to outlive their children. This was not the way the universe was supposed to work. And so we end up searching for an answer that will help us set the universe back on its axis again.

I wasn't sure if I would even say anything about God in my funeral message. After all, this wasn't a church congregation. It wasn't even a religiously affiliated school. My new community was comprised of students, staff, and faculty who were religiously diverse, non-religious, and irreligious. How would I comfort the atheist and agnostic students if I used religious language that held no meaning for them? How would I give peace to the Muslim and

1. Wis 1:13.

Hindu students if I read Christian funeral Scriptures? But how would I offer hope to the Christian students if I didn't mention the resurrection of Christ?

❧

Early on the morning of Jonathan's service, a staff person from the ROTC Department called me on behalf of the colonel. I could hear the apprehension in his voice as he asked, "Are you planning to emcee this event? The colonel is assuming you are, since funerals are more in your scope of duty than his, but we just realized we never made that clear."

"Oh, yes," I told him. "I presumed I would preside over the service, since, uh, as you say, this is something we do as clergy." *Not that I've ever done it before,* I thought to myself as I tamped down my own anxiety.

A few hours later, I was sitting with the college dignitaries on the makeshift stage in the fieldhouse, solemnly watching as close to two hundred Air Force ROTC cadets filed into the gym, lined up in formation, and then, to my dismay, stood in their lines throughout the service.

Were they not allowed to sit down?

I didn't know much about military protocol at funerals, but how could they grieve for their fellow comrade while standing up? Although they had been given the command to be "at ease," they all stayed pretty much "at attention," each one looking frozen in place.

As I looked out over all those students, they stared up at me and I recognized my own fear in their eyes.

It occurred to me then that I didn't want to be the chaplain anymore. I didn't want to be the one who had to face her own fears in order to help students move past theirs. At that moment, I thought, *I really would rather be their mother. I'd like to come down from where I'm perched with the dignitaries and hug them all, each and every one of them.*

But as they stared up at me, waiting for me to dispel the fear, I knew they didn't need me to be their mother that day. They needed me to be their chaplain.

They were no different from me, I realized, in that we were all caught up in this grip of fear, trying to come to terms with the absurd reality that death could lurk around any corner, waiting to grasp us in its clutches, ready to snatch our breath away and not give it back.

I could smell the acrid presence of fear in the room and on my own breath. I could hear the logic of fearful thoughts going through the heads of the cadets. I could see the evidence of fearful deliberation etched on their foreheads.

It seemed to say: *Jonathan was running, and Jonathan dropped dead; maybe if we keep running, we'll drop dead too; maybe we should stop running so we don't run the risk of dropping dead.*

A similar mantra was playing in my head: *Jonathan was eighteen years old, just like Wilson. Jonathan was away from home, just like Wilson. Jonathan dropped dead; maybe Wilson will drop dead too; maybe I should make Wilson come home from college so I can make sure he doesn't drop dead.*

This logic of fear held the power to seduce me to stay focused on death. I had to gather my courage, courage that members of my new community, most especially the students standing right there in front of me, had anointed me to claim.

As I looked into the eyes of the cadets, their faces transparent with both fear and hope, I received the courage to follow my fearful thoughts to where my fear was hiding—to name it, but also to name what I would lose, what we all would lose, if we let fear have the final word. That was the only way I could say words of comfort and hope and peace that would offer more than a flimsy veil of sentiment to lay over our fear. That was the only way I could move beyond my own fear and help the students move beyond theirs.

If the cadets gave in to their fear and stopped running, they'd have to quit ROTC, since running was a requirement of ROTC; and if they quit ROTC, they'd have to give up their dreams of being officers in the United States Air Force. I knew they would not want to let go of their dreams. I knew they would want to choose not to let their fear have the final word. And I didn't want to stand in the way of Wilson's dreams of going to school at Auburn, either. I didn't want fear to have the final word.

So I told the students this. I told them it was an essential thing to acknowledge our fears, spoken and unspoken, known and unknown. But we didn't have to do this alone; we could face our fears together. And then we could choose not to let fear have the final word in our lives.

We could remember how Jonathan lived rather than obsessing about how he died. We could remember what matters is not all the ways we might possibly die but all the ways we might choose how to live. We could honor Jonathan by remembering he was living into his dream of becoming an officer in the United States Air Force. We could honor him by choosing to live into our dreams, too, rather than being confined by our fear. We could do this in remembrance of him and in honor of him. This was how we could bring meaning to Jonathan's death. This was how we could bring meaning back to our lives. This was how we could help to set our universe back on its axis again.

This was how, together, we could harness the courage to face the future unafraid. Acknowledging my fears, I found, was how I would harness the courage to lean into the diverse spaces of my new community and learn not to be afraid, choosing not to let fear have the final word.

CHAPTER 2

Beer Cans in the Chapel

Practice of Nurture: Make Room for Others
Who Believe Differently

When I walked into the chapel building early on a Monday morning, I was surprised to see our department's two recycling bins filled to the brim with beer cans. My first thought was, *Did someone have a party and not invite me?*

It had been homecoming weekend, so it may have been some of the alumni. Fraternities and sororities also reserved the chapel for induction ceremonies, but it wasn't quite the time of year for that. And, anyway, they wouldn't have been drinking here. Even though we weren't a dry campus, everyone knew we had a "no alcohol" policy in the chapel building, out of respect for those who abstain due to their faith commitments. Wondering where the beer cans had come from, I made a mental note to notify the Housekeeping Department to empty the recycling bins.

I had just sat down at my desk when I looked up and saw Adam, a member of a Christian student group on campus, standing in my office doorway.

Before I could even welcome him in, he exploded. "I can't believe you would allow beer to be drunk in this sacred space! I'd like to know who did this. I bet it was one of the fraternities, wasn't it? I knew that was a bad idea letting them hold their initiation rituals, or whatever they are, here. I knew they couldn't be trusted to respect the chapel. I hope you're planning to reprimand them. What are you planning to do about it?"

I sighed inwardly. I had been *planning* to let it go.

"Adam, why don't you come in and sit down and we can talk about this?" I replied in a monotone. I didn't have the energy for this.

"I *can't,*" he insisted. "I'm on my way to class. I just stopped in to use the restroom, and when I saw all those beer cans, I thought I better bring it to your attention."

He looked at his watch, then looked over at me accusingly. "And *now* I'm late."

As if this was all my fault.

I sighed audibly this time and, feeling defeated, replied, "I'll look into it."

Satisfied he had done his duty, he turned on his heels and left.

I groaned in frustration. Students like Adam had been a thorn in my side since I began working at the college, and it had caused a lot of turmoil for me.

I thought back to the first time Adam invited me to his group's weekly meeting. I tried to be a fly on the wall among the group of thirty students, sitting in to see how they did things and to meet some of them. We were seated in a circle, and after singing some songs, the leader read some Scripture and then began a discussion. Somehow the conversation veered off topic to evolution.

And then it went down a rabbit trail.

As I listened, one student after another after another, each more animated than the last, talked about why they didn't believe in evolution.

I looked around the room. *Did everyone here believe this way?*

I couldn't tell if they did. But I couldn't tell if they didn't, either.

The conversation shifted when one of the students began talking about those who *do* believe in evolution. Others joined in, and before long it sounded like a rant.

I looked around again.

The consensus seemed to be that they could not understand how people could believe in evolution and still call themselves Christian.

My hands were clammy. *They're talking about me*, I thought.

I sat there, silent and indecisive, wondering, *Should I speak up and declare that science and faith don't have to be mutually exclusive? Should I maybe tell them about Erick?*

Erick was a second-year meteorology major who had stopped by my office one afternoon, indignant about a situation that had occurred in his weather class earlier that day.

"We were watching this film about the big bang theory," he said, "and when the film was over, I asked the professor if we could also watch a film on creationism so we could learn more than one theory on how the world came to be. He told me this is a science class and that if I want to study theology, I should go to seminary. He wouldn't even consider the idea of looking at a different theory. Can you believe that?"

Yes, I could, actually.

But I didn't say that. Instead I thought about my words and then, in what I hoped passed as a diplomatic tone, offered, "Well, he does have a point that your class is a science class, and the big bang theory *is* a scientific theory."

Maybe I imagined it, but Erick seemed to puff out his chest at my remark.

He retorted, "Yeah, but it's not the *only* theory. He should at least teach our class about *all* the theories out there."

I continued with my diplomatic tact. "I'm not sure creationism is considered a scientific theory. Isn't it a theological theory? A Christian theological theory?"

Erick narrowed his eyes and asked, "What's your point?"

Hmmm. Maybe I should take a different approach. So I said, "Erick, you're a meteorology major, right?"

He nodded.

"Can you tell me how rainbows appear in the sky?"

"Well, of course," he said, and proceeded to provide me with a detailed explanation about prisms and light and angles. Although I couldn't quite follow it all, I was convinced he understood the science behind a rainbow.

Finally, he finished. Then he asked, "Wait, what does this have to do with my class today?"

I deferred his question and pressed on. "Do you remember the story in the Bible about Noah and the flood and how after the flood, there was a rainbow?"[1]

"Sure I do."

"Do you also remember that the Bible says God put the rainbow in the clouds as a sign of God's promise never to flood the entire earth again?"

"Yeah."

"Knowing what you know about meteorology and what causes rainbows to appear, do you think that God actually placed the rainbow in the clouds?"

He thought about this. "Well . . . no," he said. "There's a scientific explanation for how the rainbow got there." He paused, his brow furrowed, then continued. "But God could still use the rainbow as a sign of God's promise never to flood the earth again."

"So you can believe what you know to be true about the science of rainbows while at the same time still believe God's promise? You don't have to take it literally for it to still be true, to still hold meaning for you?"

Erick sat there for a minute, then said, "Yeah . . . I guess so."

I watched as he connected the dots in his head.

Finally he said, "Maybe I *can* believe in the big bang theory and still believe God is the Creator of the universe."

Back in the room with Adam's group, I wanted to tell them about Erick. I wanted to tell them what Erick shared with me on a subsequent visit—how he was discovering he could hold science and the Bible together, instead of holding them apart from or against one another, and all the new discoveries he was making because of this.

1. The story of Noah, the flood, and the rainbow is found in Gen 6:9—9:17.

13

I wanted to share this with the group, but I ended up not saying a word. Instead, I shrunk into myself and hoped they didn't ask me to participate in the discussion. I justified my silence by deciding that sitting as a guest in a roomful of people who believed differently than me was not the place for me to raise questions about their beliefs, especially when they had not asked my opinion. Especially when they assumed I believed the same way.

Underneath all my justification, though, lay my desire to fit in. And to fit in, I couldn't let them know I believed differently than they did.

It only got worse when the group's officers asked me to be their staff advisor. Against my better judgment I said yes; I was afraid they would alienate me if I said no.

Once I said yes, I decided I would attend the weekly officers' meetings. I thought I could have the most influence there, since the officers were the ones who decided the direction of the group. In these meetings, I kept a lot of my beliefs to myself, but over the semester I gradually challenged the students to be more open to different perspectives and different theological beliefs. This ended up creating a lot of tension, but none of the students addressed their growing discomfort—so neither did I.

We were deep into the semester when we reached the boiling point.

At the upcoming officers' meeting, the students were planning to nominate officers for the next academic year. I was excited about this meeting, as I hoped I might encourage them to select students who were more open-minded.

But the day before the meeting, I received an email from one of the officers. He wrote, "Just wanted to let you know that tomorrow's meeting is a closed meeting, students only. Wasn't sure if you were aware that staff advisors are not to attend meetings where new officers are being chosen."

This didn't make any sense to me.

I shot off a quick reply to ask why and received an answer almost immediately. "Student Activities Department policy," was all he wrote.

Surely this wasn't true?

I called the Student Activities Department to speak with my colleague who oversaw all the student clubs on campus.

"Jennifer, hi, this is Melynne," I said when she answered. "I've got a question. Is there a policy that states staff advisors are not to attend an officers' meeting when the students choose new officers for their club?"

Jennifer sounded surprised. "What? No, not at all. Actually, we like the staff advisors to be there so they can be a sounding board as the officers deliberate. Where did you get the idea you shouldn't be there?"

"The students told me it was your department's policy for all the clubs."

There was a beat too long of silence on the other end. In that moment, we both realized what had happened.

Then I heard Jennifer say, "Oh. Wow. That's not right."

"No . . . no, it isn't," I quietly agreed.

I thanked her for her help, hung up, and sat at my desk, numb.

They lied to me.

I was stunned.

They lied to me.

I was livid.

They lied to me.

Underneath it all, I was deeply wounded. I had so wanted to fit in. But I knew I would never belong unless I could believe like they did—something they had assumed I did in the beginning but then realized wasn't true.

I wrote an email to all the officers, outlining what had transpired and requesting they meet with me. No one replied.

Late that afternoon I was preparing to leave for the day when Rafael, one of the officers, tapped lightly on the open door of my office. He looked distraught.

I was in no mood to talk. I curtly said, "Rafael, I'm about to leave for the day. Maybe you could stop by tomorrow during my office hours."

"I'm sorry I couldn't get here sooner, but I really need to talk to you *now*," he replied. And with that, he shut the door, sat down, and burst out, "I had no idea you were told not to come to the meeting tomorrow until I received your email. I don't even know which officers knew and which didn't. But it doesn't matter. I can't believe any of them would lie to you. They're supposed to be my friends, my *Christian* friends, and I don't even feel like I know who they are. I mean, yeah, I know we all believe differently than you do, but that doesn't mean we shouldn't treat you with respect. I don't even know if I want to be an officer anymore. I don't even know if I want to be associated with this group anymore."

"Well, that makes two of us." The words were out of my mouth before I knew they were even on my tongue. I immediately sought to rectify it. "I'm sorry, Rafael. That was not appropriate for me to say. It's been a hard day. I guess what I mean to say is that I think I should resign as the group's advisor."

"I don't blame you," Rafael responded. "I still can't believe they treated you this way."

I nodded and went on, "I appreciate you coming to see me. And I want you to know how much I have appreciated you making room for me in the officers' meetings when the others would shoot down ideas I suggested. I think you have a lot to offer the group."

I resigned as the group's advisor. I told myself it would be best for all concerned, but I wasn't sure if my motives were altruistic, revengeful, or a way to protect my tender feelings.

I had thought I would love the freedom I associated with being a chaplain, the freedom to be true to who I am theologically and relationally. A chaplain was not supposed to have an agenda, an ulterior motive of getting people to change in some way. Rather, the expectation was on me to honor each person I encountered, regardless of his or her faith identity or belief system or behavior toward me. I wanted to value people by virtue of their humanity and not because of what they believed or how they behaved or what they looked like or where they came from. I believed the essence of my calling as a chaplain was to reflect God's unconditional acceptance of us by accepting others this way.

This was why I had such a hard time with the religious students whose behavior pointed to a conditional God. I wanted them to know that God's acceptance of us was not conditional. I felt passionate about this—and I knew my passion stemmed back to my childhood.

❧

When I was a little girl, my family didn't go to church. But almost every summer we traveled back home to my grandmother's farm in northern Louisiana, where I went with her to the old country church down the road. It was a small white clapboard building sitting next to the graveyard, keeping company with the departed members. It was a humble structure, unassuming with no steeple. Visitors passing by might not have realized it was a church except for the sign declaring it so: Boeuf Prairie Methodist Church. Inside, the worn wooden pews, faded hymnals, and ancient scent bore witness to the hundred-plus years of its existence.

I thought of that church as God's house, but I knew God didn't hang out only there; she followed my grandmother everywhere she went. Mamaw was my first memory of God—someone who kept me safe, wrapped her warm, loving arms around me, and enfolded me into her bosom just because she delighted in my presence. I used to think I was her favorite until I realized she loved the other eleven cousins the same way she loved me. I considered myself fortunate that her love was big enough for all of us.

Mamaw's God was an up-close, not-afraid-to-get-her-hands-dirty kind of God; she fed me biscuits and fried chicken, saved me from the black snake slithering too close for comfort, and forgave me when I hid my black-eyed peas—the ones she had grown, picked, shelled, and boiled—in my iced tea because I didn't like the mealy way they tasted. She even cared about the dogs, gathering the scraps from our plates and setting them outside in a pie tin for the strays that came around. I knew in the marrow of my bones that Mamaw's God loved me. In the deepest part of my spirit, I knew I was lovable.

Not long after I turned fourteen, I went with some kids from my neighborhood to a church youth group and heard about a God whose son had to die because of me. A God who could not be in my presence and was not delighted in me. They told me I was bad and that only Jesus dying on the cross could make me good. Only Jesus could bring me back to God.

This did not sound like my grandmother's God, the God who showed up everywhere, even on Mamaw's back porch; the God who wrapped her arms around me and drew me close. This new God sounded distant and harsh, like a judge sitting way up on a throne with a gavel, pronouncing me guilty. But if I did the right thing and accepted Jesus into my heart, then I would not get punished and end up in hell.

There was a palpable difference between the unconditional love of my grandmother's God and the conditional love of the youth group's God. It didn't make sense to me that if I said a few abstract words, a simple prayer, then God would accept me. I didn't have to say anything to be accepted and loved by Mamaw's God.

But Mamaw's God was a thousand miles away, and I wanted to be a part of the youth group. Here, too, I wanted to belong. So I kept my questions to myself and said the right words, the words I had been told to say. I accepted Jesus into my heart, and then I was told I was now acceptable to enter God's presence; I could go to heaven after I die.

I had hoped against all hope that once I said the right words, I would feel the same way I had felt back on my grandmother's farm. But I didn't. My suspicions were confirmed. Saying the right words might be enough to get into heaven, but it wasn't going to be enough to get back to Mamaw's God.

Now that I knew God set conditions, I recognized I would not only have to say the right words; I would also have to do the right things if I was going to get God to love me the way she loved me back at Mamaw's house. I was going to have to figure out what pleased God and then make sure I did those things.

This was nothing new to me; it was the way the rest of my life had already been laid out. My parents were satisfied with me when

I behaved the way they told me to; they were not so placated when I rebelled. My teachers were pleased when I made good grades but disappointed in me if I let them slip. My friends included me in their activities when I went along with their plans but shunned me if I questioned too much. And I had a hunch my youth group leaders would not be as interested in me if I were not interested in their God.

My young self was perceptive enough to understand that love and acceptance by others is naturally conditional. Why would I have thought God was any different?

So I grew into adulthood working hard to earn and keep the approval of others, including God. As a result, I lost my sense of self. I also lost my memory of Mamaw's God.

By the time I reached my early thirties, the burden had become so heavy that I finally crumbled beneath its weight. Living a false self for so many years—decades, really—had taken its toll on me physically, mentally, and spiritually. I went to see a counselor, and together we ever so slowly dismantled my self and put me back together again. It was a daunting process, one that required peeling off and sifting through layer after layer—all the detritus and the dung—to get down to the core of who I was. But in the end it was exhilarating, as I discovered my inquisitive, sensitive, lovable self.

And that was when I began to remember my grandmother's God.

I remembered how I felt at Mamaw's house, the unconditional love and acceptance of Mamaw's God. The way she delighted in me and drew me close to her; how she nurtured me and saved me and forgave me. And finally, *finally*, I could hear God calling me *Beloved* once again.

I began to re-discover the relational faith I had once known. I began to understand Scripture as a story of God interacting with humanity, interacting with *me*, rather than a guidebook of dos and don'ts.

Eventually, this led me to seminary, and it wasn't too long until I started questioning the popular understanding of the atonement, the one that said Christ paid the penalty for my sins so I

19

could be reconciled to God and go to heaven after I die. This was the understanding of God the youth group had introduced to me, an understanding that led to faith in a conditional God. This was the understanding of God that this young man Adam claimed, which he expressed by following a moral code, a set of rules of what he believed was acceptable to God.

As I explored further in my seminary studies, I learned there is more than one way to understand atonement. I was pleased to discover the various other ways that Christians down through the centuries have believed in the significance of Christ's death, ways that point to the unconditional love of God, to a relational God rather than a transactional God, a God who nurtures and saves and forgives us freely, with no strings attached.

❦

After leaving messages with all the student groups that might have used the chapel over the weekend, I got to the bottom of the beer cans mystery late that afternoon when Stephen, the student president of the Catholic ministry on campus, knocked on my open door.

"Hi, Stephen," I said, "Come on in."

He walked in and said, "I got your message about the beer cans in the recycling bins and wanted to come talk to you about it."

"Oh? Do you know something about it?" I asked, gesturing for him to sit down.

He sat in one of my armchairs, and I came from around my desk and sat in the other.

He said, "We're the ones who put the beer cans in the recycling bins."

I could feel my eyes bulge in their sockets. "I . . . I . . . I'm . . . I'm . . . sh . . . shocked," I stammered, then recovered enough to formulate a complete sentence. "I can't believe it." Although I knew the Catholic students drank (they even had a "Theology on Tap" discussion group at the local bar), they had always been respectful.

I would never have imagined they would be the ones to go against our policy.

"But we weren't drinking here," he said.

I gave him a dubious stare.

"Let me explain," he continued, and blurted out the rest of his story. "We needed empty aluminum cans for our homecoming float and had asked all our members to save their cans and bring them in. Once we started working on the float, we realized we didn't need as many cans as we thought, so we just put the leftovers in the recycling bins. We didn't even think anything about it. I guess it was because the beer cans we brought in were empty."

I laughed. "Of all the possible scenarios, I never would have been able to guess that this is how the cans got there. I'm really glad you came in and let me know."

"I'm so glad you're not upset with us," Stephen said. "I talked with some of the other members, and we all want you to know how very sorry we are that we didn't think about how it would look to throw the beer cans in the bins. I hope you know we would never drink in the chapel. We want to be respectful of those who don't drink."

After Stephen left, I thought back to how the day had started and how it had ended. What a difference between Stephen and Adam. Stephen so gracious, and Adam so . . . well, ungracious.

Then another thought came unbidden.

What a difference between Stephen and me.

I allowed myself to digest this. Stephen understood that just because the Catholic students believed it was okay to drink, that didn't mean others needed to believe the same way. He made room for Adam to believe differently—but Adam made no room for anyone who didn't believe like him.

I thought I made room for people who believed differently, too. But after listening to Stephen, I was hit with the reality that I hadn't made room for Adam or for others who believed like him. I wanted Adam to believe like me. I wanted him to believe in a God who loves us unconditionally, and I wanted him to treat others in a way that would reflect the unconditional acceptance of God. But I didn't want to treat *him* that way.

I am no different than Adam.

I was reminded of my vow as a chaplain: to honor each person I encountered regardless of his or her faith identity or belief system or behavior toward me, to value them by virtue of their humanity and not because of what they believed or how they behaved or what they looked like or where they came from; to reflect God's unconditional acceptance of us by accepting others this way.

Why had I not seen I hadn't kept this vow toward Adam and the others who believed like him? Was it because I had already stereotyped them, which made it easy for me to lump them altogether into a problem I had to deal with rather than seeing them as individuals to connect with? Maybe it was also because Adam reminded me of my younger self, when I had a black-and-white faith. A wise mentor once shared with me that the people we have the hardest time with are often those who remind us of the parts of ourselves we would rather choose to forget.

In my denomination, we take both provisional and permanent vows as ordained clergy. I had been provisionally ordained before I started at the college and then was permanently ordained while working there.

The night of my ordination service, when I knelt on my knees with the bishop's hand on my head and his words in my ears, I became strangely aware of some kind of presence hovering nearby. I was reminded of the Scripture passage about our ancestors in the faith, the great cloud of witnesses surrounding us.[2] And then, with startling clarity, I knew the spirit of my grandmother was with me in that sanctuary.

I imagined that long ago in a very different time and place, probably at the edge of a cotton field on the prairie of northern

2. See Heb 11:1—12:1.

Louisiana, she, too, had knelt on her knees to be ordained by God, pledging her life to love others the way God loved her.

I scooted over a smidgen to make room for Mamaw's spirit to abide with me as I reaffirmed my vows to love others the way God loved me. And to make room for those who believed differently.

CHAPTER 3

The Invitation

Practice of Nurture: Create a Safe Space

Something shifted in me the night I sat in the campus auditorium watching a documentary on the life and death of a young gay man. I probably would not have gone to watch the film except that I had been asked to lead the vigil afterward; I thought it would be disrespectful if I did the one and didn't show up for the other. Nonetheless, I was uncomfortable, as I thought I would be.

Isaac, a student involved with the Gay Straight Alliance, a student group on campus, had come to my office and asked if I would help him and his group organize a vigil. It was to commemorate the first anniversary of the death of Ryan Skipper, a young man from Polk County, Florida (less than two hours from campus), who had been bullied, beaten, and murdered because he was gay. Isaac told me their plan: to show a documentary that had been made about Ryan, titled *Accessory to Murder: Our Culture's Complicity in the Death of Ryan Skipper*; and after the film, to invite the audience to walk from the auditorium to the campus chapel for a vigil, where we would honor and remember Ryan and others who had been victims of hate crimes. Isaac and the other members of the GSA wanted this event to raise awareness on campus about the prejudice against LGBTQ students and to promote tolerance.

I wanted to say yes. I wanted to stand up for these students and for those who had died. My heart told me to do this. But I was afraid. I was still a relatively new clergyperson ordained in a denomination that was wishy-washy about the issue of homosexuality.

On the one hand, the denomination's policy book declared the practice of homosexuality to be "incompatible with Christian teaching."[1] Many had been trying to get this statement deleted because it was not consistent with the denomination's commitment to a contextual reading of Scripture; and as a result, it legitimized discrimination of LGBTQ persons. On the other hand, the policy book also claimed, "All persons, regardless of . . . sexual orientation, are entitled to have their human and civil rights ensured and to be protected against violence."[2]

These conflicting statements reflected an ongoing debate in my denomination between those who took a moral stance against homosexuality and those who took an ethical stance toward treating LGBTQ persons with the dignity and respect they deserve as human beings.

And then there were some who tried to keep a foot in both camps by distinguishing between sexual identity and sexual practice, saying, essentially, "Who you are is okay, but what you're doing is not." This only revealed their lack of understanding that a LGBTQ person is no different from a straight person when it comes to love. They both want to find someone with whom they can fall in love who will love them for who they are, someone with whom they might be able to share the rest of their life in mutual love, support, and companionship in marriage. They know sexual intimacy, in its truest sense, is an expression of love and therefore has the potential to transcend physical connection to embrace the depths of emotional and spiritual union. To tell LGBTQ persons that it is wrong for them to have the same intimacy that is considered normal, healthy, and expected in a heterosexual couple's marriage is to send the message they are inferior to straight persons.

1. *Book of Discipline*, 103.
2. *Book of Discipline*, 103.

I thought I knew what I believed about all this—but I didn't know what my clergy supervisors believed. How would they react if I participated in this event?

I had another reason to be afraid. So many religious students on campus—and staff and faculty, too—held conservative views, and they assumed, even expected, that I shared their perspective. As the relatively new chaplain, I wanted everyone to accept me, so I had kept silent about my beliefs on controversial issues. I didn't think anyone on campus really knew where I stood on the issue of homosexuality. I was concerned if they knew I held more liberal theological views, they would reject me.

Surely Isaac had no idea what my views were. In fact, I wondered why he had come to see me in the first place. How was it he was able to take a leap of faith and trust me rather than stereotype me as one of those religious professionals who spurned LGBTQ persons?

I wanted Isaac and the other LGBTQ students to know I supported them. I wanted them to know I didn't take literally the alleged biblical directives against homosexuality. How could I? My identity as a clergywoman was an embodiment of that same contextual reading of Scripture. Read in context, the Bible reveals numerous ways women were empowered to be spiritual leaders; a literal reading ignores, overlooks, or dismisses this, which is why some churches forbid women to be ordained. I didn't let individual verses speak for themselves; I read and interpreted them in light of the whole context of the Bible as well as the historical contexts in which the Bible was written.

Maybe this was why Isaac thought he could trust me. Maybe he was astute enough to recognize my identity as a clergywoman implied my contextual reading of Scripture. Perhaps he already knew I didn't take the Bible literally.

My gut told me to do it, to advocate for these students by helping with the vigil. To be true to myself—*to be true to these students*—was to say yes. But it would expose me to others, and I wasn't sure I was ready to do that.

I also knew, however, that the event was not about me. It was about people being accepted and loved for who they are as human beings. It was about proclaiming God loves us, all of us, whether we are LGBTQ or straight. Why would I want to keep silent about that?

Why *had* I kept silent about that?

I was reminded of a conversation with one of my clergy colleagues who had shared with me his long and difficult journey toward claiming his identity as a gay man. He gradually uncovered the layered realization that he would never be his authentic self until he accepted his God-given sexual identity. I remembered thinking at the time, *I am no different than him, yearning to be my authentic self and the arduous journey it takes to get there.*

And so I told Isaac yes. It was an anxious yes. A timid yes. A yes that left me feeling awkward and exposed as I leaned into claiming what I believed.

ॐ

As I watched the film that night in the campus auditorium—listening to Ryan's friends and family talk about Ryan and how much they loved him because he was Ryan and how much others despised him because he was gay—I began to feel a heaviness in my chest. Then came a dawning awareness that right there, in that auditorium, were young men and women who knew firsthand the same kind of prejudice and bullying depicted in the film.

I'm worried about my reputation, and they are worried about their very lives.

I had not paid attention to how marginalized the LGBTQ community was, not only by the church, but also by the culture at large. How had I contributed to their marginalization? How had I been complicit? How had my ignorance and naiveté—*my silence*—caused them harm? Something shifted in me as I sat there, and I recognized that the heaviness in my heart was the weight of conviction. Another thought began to rise up to my consciousness: *Forgive me for the things I have done and for the things I have left undone. Forgive me for the words I have said and for the words I have left unsaid.*

After the documentary ended, we solemnly walked from the auditorium to the chapel, where I led the vigil. Isaac and some of the other students had displayed poster-sized photographs of young men and women who, like Ryan, had been murdered because of their sexual identity. They also had created a video that told the story, the life and death, of each person.

Ryan Skipper's parents were in attendance, as were many others who were grieving the loss of loved ones who had been killed because of their sexual identity. We watched the video, we sang songs, we cried, we laughed, and we lit candles to honor and remember these lives that had been snuffed out way too soon. The sanctuary was full of students who shared words of their loss. They also shared their hopes and dreams of a culture where all people are treated with respect and dignity, where all people are honored. Where all people feel safe enough to be their authentic selves.

By the end of the vigil, I felt the unconditional love the people in that room had not just for one another, I realized, but for me too. I felt prompted to cast aside my scripted closing remarks and instead share a little of what I experienced that evening. I concluded by telling those gathered, "I want each of you to know that this sanctuary is a safe place for you. If you are looking for somewhere to rest in your weariness, to set down your burden for a little while and be who you are, this is a safe place for you to do that. If you have given up on God, or on all that is sacred, because of the people who have given up on you, I want you to know that this is a safe place to seek the sacred without scrutiny from others. And just as Isaac and the rest of you have created a safe space for me and others like me here tonight, it is my desire, my hope, and my prayer that I might become a sanctuary, too, a safe space for you."

May I no longer be complicit in death; may I be a sanctuary for the preservation and flourishing of life.

૨૬

A year or so after the vigil, as the Gay Straight Alliance (renamed PRIDE, which stood for People Respecting Identity, Diversity, and Equality) prepared to host a conference for all the college PRIDE groups across the state, the college received word that Westboro Baptist Church, a hate group that insists God abhors gays, would be coming to town to protest during the conference. The director of the Student Activities Department suggested I write an article for the campus newspaper to "counter-protest" the Westboro group and send a message of love to the students.

His suggestion resonated with me. I knew I wasn't an activist, someone who would walk the streets holding a sign in counter-protest. But I knew I could be an advocate; that was more in keeping with who I am. And I could support these students by doing what came naturally to me: writing. So I wrote the counter-protest article:

> *The Westboro Baptist Church is reportedly planning to picket the Florida Collegiate PRIDE Conference this weekend because they claim that God hates gays. Their view of God's love is one which says God's love is limited, that God's love does not extend to everyone. The Westboro group certainly is not the first to put limits on God's love, and they won't be the last. But their view is not the only view of God's love.*
>
> *Another view is one that says God's love has no limits, that it extends to everyone and that as much as we might like to exclude some groups of people from God's love that no one is beyond the bounds of that love. No one. This view claims that God's love is not based on one's sexual identity any more than it is based on one's ethnicity or gender. It's not even based on one's moral behavior (or lack thereof) or even one's religious belief. This view says God's love for people is based solely on our identity as human beings, and the dignity and respect that such identity entails.*
>
> *It can be a powerful blessing when people look beyond our labels and see us as human beings, even more so when people treat us with dignity and respect because of it. May*

each and every attendee at the conference next weekend receive this blessing.

I wanted the students attending the conference to know they are loved just as they are. I wanted to create a safe space for them to be their authentic selves—just like Isaac had created a safe space for me to be my authentic self.

CHAPTER 4

Am I Enough?

Practice of Nurture: Embrace Your Worthiness

I INHERITED A SUNDAY morning chapel service when I began working as the college chaplain. My predecessor had inherited it too. To my knowledge, no one had ever questioned its existence. Each semester, attendance would start off with about twenty to twenty-five students, mostly freshmen; then the numbers would steadily dwindle over the course of the semester until it leveled off at about ten students for the last month or so.

I struggled to find ways to keep the students there and to increase the attendance. I advertised. I changed the name. I brought in bagels and donuts every week. But each semester was the same. I always wondered where the students went.

My first thought, of course, was that they didn't like my preaching. My second thought was that they decided to sleep in—that they started the semester with good intentions but that one thing led to another and by the time Sunday came around, they were too tired. Or perhaps they'd lost interest in faith-related activities altogether, especially with so many other things on campus vying for their attention.

Then one afternoon I ran into Kali as I walked across campus to Starbucks for an iced tea. Kali had come the first couple of

Sundays of the semester but had not attended since. I wasn't sure what to say when I saw her; all I could think about were the things I didn't want to say—the things I always hear when I'm away from my home church for a stretch. Things like, *We haven't seen you here in a while. Where have you been? We've missed seeing you.* I guess church members think they mean well, but it always comes off as a cross-examination. I didn't want to do the same thing to Kali, so I just said hi and asked how things were going for her.

"Really well," she replied. "My classes are good, and I tried out for the club volleyball team and made it, so that's been fun. Oh, and I started going to a church not far from here. One of the students I met at your chapel service gives me a ride every week. That's why we're not there anymore. We both really wanted to find a church home."

Interesting.

Here I thought it had something to do with me. Or that she'd been lazy or disinterested.

"That's great, Kali!" I said. "I'm so glad you've found a church you can call home while you're here."

The more I got out of my office and walked the campus, the more I ran into these "chapel dropouts." I learned most of them were attending churches off campus; many of them, like Kali, had found a church home. Although at first I felt slightly dismissed that they would rather go to a church in the community than the service on campus, I soon realized I didn't need to compete. The chapel service was not church; it was a convenient place to go until students could figure out where they wanted to go to church.

When I really thought about it, I liked the idea of the students going to a real, bona fide church. It would be good for them to have the opportunity to get involved in the life of a local church community and connect with people of other ages who shared their faith. It made sense to me that if they got involved in a church while in college, they would be more likely to continue to be involved in church after college.

All of this made me wonder if having a chapel service on campus was a good idea at all. If most of the students who attended the chapel service were looking for a church, why should I bother with all the time and effort to hold a chapel service every week? Why didn't I just skip that step and help them find a church home?

I began to wonder if the chapel service did a disservice to the few students who were regulars. If we didn't have a service on campus, would they go looking for a church off campus? When I queried them, the majority said yes.

The bottom line was that most students who were interested in a worship service were also interested in being a part of a local church community. The more I thought about it, the more I knew discontinuing the service was the right thing to do.

I began to consider what it would be like not to have the chapel service as one of my primary responsibilities; it took a lot of time and energy to prepare for each week, and was geared toward only the Protestant Christian students at the college. I'd been hired to work primarily with these students because this was what the volunteer chaplains before me had done. But I wasn't a volunteer. I was the first employed chaplain at this religiously diverse secular college. Perhaps it would be more equitable to spend my time working for all the students rather than a particular subset, as had been done in the past.

The more I thought about it, the more inspired I became about broadening the vision of the chaplaincy office. It would help create a campus culture where every person, regardless of their faith identity, could feel welcome on the campus, knowing this was a safe place for them to be who they were and that they didn't have to hide their religious identity.

I talked with my supervisor, and he got on board, so we made plans to discontinue the service at the end of the school year.

But I couldn't stop the nagging thought that I had somehow failed.

I knew I had done everything I possibly could have done for the chapel service to succeed, but I kept thinking of what else I might have tried. Much as I wanted to put it out of my mind, the pesky thoughts clung to me until I became aware of other thoughts buried deeper.

If only I was younger—twenty-five or even thirty or thirty-five, instead of forty-five—I could have made it work.

Then another: *If only I was a more dynamic preacher, someone who moves around and gets excited, I could have made it succeed.*

Then one more: *Probably if I was a man, it would have worked. If only I was a thirty-something extroverted male instead of a forty-something introverted female, it would have thrived.*

In other words, if I could have been someone I am not, perhaps the service would have flourished.

I'm not any different than my students, I realized.

Students came into my office all the time wrestling with decisions that ultimately were about trying to be someone they were not, trying to keep up with someone else's standard of who they should be, trying to be *enough*. Somehow they heard subtle messages, just like I did, that who they were was not enough.

Natalie was one such student. A twenty-five-year-old first-year student who had spent the last six years in the US Army (half of those years in Iraq), she came to see me toward the end of her first year.

"I've spent a year trying to fit in at this school, and it's not working," she said. "I don't know what's wrong with me."

I asked her to tell me a little more.

"I don't fit into the culture here—the military culture, the aerospace and aviation culture, the conservative political culture, the corporate culture. The students here seem to have a superior attitude, like they're better than everyone else. The ROTC students, instead of wanting to learn from the experiences of some of us veterans, think they know more than us because they'll be officers and we were enlisted. They romanticize the military and make it sound like it's some kind of elite club. It's like they've completely forgotten the mission of the military is to defend the country. Meanwhile, all of us vets, who actually *have* defended the country, are coming out of it with broken bodies and broken spirits."

I took a second to decide how I wanted to respond, but Natalie wasn't finished.

"And then the students majoring in aerospace engineering have a certain kind of arrogance about them. It's like an aura, like they're so much smarter than the rest of us. I mean, I know they're the ones who'll be the astronauts and the rocket scientists, but still."

She cleared her throat and went on.

"And the aeronautical science majors have this swagger to them, like they think they're better than the rest of us because they'll be the ones flying the big jets one day. Who cares? Airline pilots are just glorified taxi drivers in the sky anyway."

I didn't know what to say. But I didn't need to say anything yet because Natalie took a breath and kept going.

"What's wrong with me?" she asked, her voice turning hoarse. "Everyone here thinks this school is top-notch, and they love being here among other students who think like they do. Even the veterans love being here."

Her shoulders sagged and her voice trickled down to almost a whisper. I had to lean forward to hear her.

"I just don't fit in," she said. "Sometimes I feel like being here is eroding my spirit."

Those words touched a place deep within me.

She wiped at her eyes, and I gave her space to collect herself, then asked, "Natalie, how did you decide to come to this college? What was it that stood out for you?"

"I guess I was following all the other vets who came to school here," she replied. "I figured I should do something related to what I did in the army. But I didn't get to pick what I did in the army; they assigned our jobs to us.

"It's hard to know what to do when, for six years, someone else tells you what to do. They're basically telling you who you are. It's hard when, all of a sudden, you have the freedom to choose for yourself.

"I guess it felt like too much freedom—too many choices. So I chose something that didn't seem too far off from what I knew in the army. It seemed like a good fit for all the other vets I knew. I don't know why it's not a good fit for me. What's wrong with me?"

There was that question again. It reminded me of all the times I had asked it of myself. I chose my words carefully.

"Natalie, sometimes when we try to fit ourselves into something that's not a good fit for us," I began, "or when we compare our experience to someone else's and don't feel like ours measures up, or when others tell us who we are instead of allowing us to claim that for ourselves, we end up feeling like something must be wrong with us. But I don't think anything is wrong with you."

She waited for me to say more.

I weighed whether to say what else I was thinking, then went ahead with it. "It sounds like *this school* might not be the right fit for you."

Natalie's eyes widened. "You think I should leave?" she asked.

I went on. "Let me ask you a question. If you let go of what you think you should be doing and where you think you should be going to school, and instead embrace the freedom to study anything you want and go to school anywhere you want, what do you think you would do?"

She thought about it. "I'd love to study sociology and eventually become a licensed social worker. I think I'd like to help some of the young vets who have PTSD. And I'd love to go to a school where I can be around people who are thinking about some of the big questions of life and not about the military and airplanes and rockets all the time."

"Natalie, it sounds like maybe a small liberal arts college might be a better fit for you," I said.

She was surprised I would suggest that she transfer. But I did because I thought it would be the best thing for her. I did because I felt like she was describing *me* when she said she didn't fit in. I felt like I didn't fit in, either, and I often felt like something was wrong with me because of it. I wished I could transfer and be the chaplain at a small liberal arts college. That would be a better fit for who I was. Natalie was the first person who had put into words the kind of angst I had been feeling.

Maybe being here is eroding my spirit.

Natalie did end up transferring to a small liberal arts college. The following year, I ran into her while attending a conference in the same town as her new school. She looked radiant. She said transferring was the best decision she could have ever made. She loved it because she could be herself and finally felt at home in her own skin.

ॐ

Similarly, Travis came to see me the second week of the first semester of his freshman year. He was from Wyoming and said he was homesick and thought he'd made a huge mistake coming all the way across the country. He wanted to go home and said he should have gone to our sister school in Arizona, which would have been closer to his home in Wyoming. I asked why he'd decided not to go there originally; he said he'd thought he wanted to be in Navy ROTC, and they didn't have a program for the navy at our sister school.

"Travis, if you transfer to our sister school, then you do realize you won't be able to be in Navy ROTC, don't you?" I asked.

He nodded. "That's okay. Now that I've done it for the past week, I'm not so sure I want to be in it anymore."

"Oh?"

"I'm not sure what I thought it would be like, but it's not what I had imagined it would be. For one thing, we have to run every morning. I don't even like to exercise. I don't know what I was thinking."

"What made you think you had wanted to be in it in the first place?"

"My dad was in the navy when he was younger, and that's all he ever talked about. I thought it would make him proud if I went into the navy too."

His words took me back to when I was in my twenties and joined the Army Reserves. At the time, I thought it would make my dad, a career military officer, proud of me. It was much later in life that I realized I had been trying to prove my worth to him.

Travis continued, "I don't see my dad too much because my parents are divorced. He was so excited when I told him I was going to be in Navy ROTC. I think he would be really disappointed if I dropped out."

He was silent for a few minutes and seemed to be in deep thought.

I waited.

Finally he said, "But if I transfer to the school in Arizona to be closer to home, it won't be like I dropped out of Navy ROTC because I wanted to. It would be because the school doesn't offer it."

I thought about this and then said, "Travis, if you didn't have to worry about how your dad feels about you doing ROTC, would you rather go to school here or in Arizona?"

Without a second's hesitation, he said, "I'd much rather stay here."

I was surprised, given what he'd said about being homesick. "How come you'd rather stay here?" I asked.

"I've lived my whole life in the same small town in Wyoming," he sighed. "I've gone to school with the same people from kindergarten through high school. Most of the ones who are going to college from my class are either going to the community college in town or the state college about an hour away. If I stayed there, that's what I would be doing too. There's nothing wrong with that, but I wanted something different. I wanted to go to college far away and experience a different part of the country, rather than continuing to live my life the same way as everyone else. I wanted to go somewhere where I didn't know anyone, where I could meet new people and have new experiences."

He looked down, frowning. "I had big dreams for myself."

We were both silent for a little while.

Then I softly asked, "So, would you say the priority in your desire to transfer is because you are homesick or because you want to get out of ROTC?"

"Well, I mean, I *am* homesick," he said. "But I guess the real reason is because I want to get out of ROTC."

"And since they don't have a Navy ROTC program at the Arizona school, you wouldn't have to disappoint your dad," I added.

He nodded.

"Travis, you have taken a huge leap of faith to come all the way across the country to begin living out the dreams you have for yourself," I said. "Have you thought about the possibility that you may disappoint yourself if you don't stay here?"

Travis's brow furrowed. "I hadn't really thought of it like that. But, yeah, it would be a huge disappointment to give up my dream of going to school here. Maybe a bigger disappointment than disappointing my dad."

Travis's need for recognition and approval from his dad reminded me of my own need for recognition and approval from my dad all those years ago. It also connected with a more recent struggle I'd had as a minister.

In the United Methodist Church, the two different tracks of ordained ministry, elders and deacons, are supposed to be equal but distinct ways to live out the ministry of the ordained. But in reality, elders are often seen as higher up, further along than deacons.

When I began my ordination process, I started off on the elder track. But as I drew nearer and nearer to the time I needed to make it official, I became more and more anxious about it. Most elders are pastors of churches. They stand behind pulpits every Sunday and preach sermons. They organize the running of the church and take care of the congregation. That's not all they do, but that's a lot of what they do, and I didn't particularly feel called to any of that. I wanted to be out in the world beyond the church, encountering the sacred in the faces of strangers. I felt called to the kinds of ministries deacons are called to do—ministries of justice and peace and compassion with people from all different beliefs and walks of life.

So why was I on the elder track?

I agonized over it and finally realized I was hanging on to the elder track for the wrong reasons. I wanted to be seen the way elders are seen. I wanted the recognition and approval that comes with being an elder. Even though deacons and elders have the same credentials—the same education, the same training, the same standards for ordination—deacons' ministries tend to have less visibility and less status. Many people don't even know deacons are ordained.

But if I became an elder, I would be hindered in my ability to live out my dreams. If I became a deacon, I would be freed up to do the work I felt called to do. I would be freed up to be who I am.

That, after all, is what it came down to. I wanted to have the freedom to be who I am and to do the work I felt called to do.

In the end, Travis decided the same thing. He dropped out of ROTC and stayed at our college to pursue his dreams.

Over and over again, I watched students struggle with the same thing I struggled with and the same thing Natalie and Travis struggled with. People let us know we're not enough in so many subtle ways. Maybe it's someone's expectation that we live up to their standards. Maybe it's the history tapes from childhood that play over and over in our heads. Maybe it's the way we're dismissed because we don't choose a revered major or an esteemed career path. Or maybe it's the church that tells us we are not good enough, misleading us to believe there is no good in us unless we believe like they do.

Over time, these external messages become internalized and we don't even notice it happening. We absorb the voices of others that tell us "You are not enough" and they become mingled with our own voices until one day we wake up to find ourselves saying "*I* am not enough." It wears down our spirits, no matter how resilient we are.

When the Student Activities Department began putting together a conference for student leaders, I decided to facilitate a workshop about this "not enough" struggle. I wanted students to know they didn't have to measure up to someone else's expectations for who they should be. I wanted them to know if they paid attention to who they were and led out of their own unique identity and gifts instead of the measurements that they or others imposed on them, they would be gifted leaders.

I decided to call the workshop "You Don't Have to Be Perfect to Be a Leader" and to base it on the work of Brené Brown, a research professor at the University of Houston. But it wasn't until I prepared the material for the workshop that I realized how it spoke to my feelings of inadequacy about the chapel service. It occurred to me that maybe I needed the workshop just as much, if not more than, the students.

In her book *The Gifts of Imperfection: Let Go of Who You Think You're Supposed to Be and Embrace Who You Are*, Brown tells us we can cultivate worthiness by "practicing courage, compassion, and connection in our daily lives."[1] She defines courage as "speaking honestly and openly about who we are, about what we're feeling, and about our experiences (good and bad)."[2] She says ordinary courage is about being vulnerable. It's about owning our own stories. She also says we often don't want to acknowledge to ourselves, much less others, the things we don't like about ourselves or our feelings of disappointment—our feelings of not being good enough.

I hadn't wanted to own my feelings about the chapel service. Even though I knew discontinuing the service was the right thing to do and that it would lead to a new and exciting way of doing things, I had still felt like a failure, like somehow I wasn't enough. I had not wanted to look at those feelings, so at first I tried to ignore them. When I finally allowed myself to look at why I felt like a failure, I realized how critical I was being with myself.

Brown says that to be able to have the courage to look at our own stories, we need to practice compassion with ourselves. This means being kind to ourselves the same way we would be kind to someone else. It means realizing we're not alone in feeling we're not enough; everyone feels inadequate at times. And it means

1. Brown, *Gifts of Imperfection*, 7.
2. Brown, *Gifts of Imperfection*, 12–13.

neither denying nor dramatizing our feelings but rather accepting them and being kind toward them.[3]

Once I began to be kind toward my feelings about the chapel service, I was able to remember that my predecessor had shared the same predicament of low attendance at his chapel services, as had his predecessor (and they were both males!). I wasn't alone in the struggle of trying to get it to succeed. And it wasn't all about me. It wasn't about exaggerating my feelings or denying my feelings. It was about accepting the reality of my feelings with kindness.

Lastly, Brown describes connection as "the energy that exists between people when they feel seen, heard, and valued; when they can give and receive without judgment; and when they derive sustenance and strength from the relationship."[4] We all need people in our lives who can connect with us in this way. It had taken the chapel dropouts connecting with me in a non-defensive, non-judgmental way for me to realize they were better off attending a church home in the local community than going to a service on campus. And I was better off being able to put my energy and resources toward creating a broader way to be available to all students on campus. The campus as a whole would be better served.

I could be kind toward myself about discontinuing the chapel service. It wasn't meant to live on; it had outlived its purpose.

Even so, it took courage for me to even contemplate discontinuing a service that had been in place for decades and to take on the hard work of steering us in a new direction. But I also knew this was what the college needed—and it was the kind of work I felt called to do. I came to realize I was the right person for this next chapter in the college's spiritual life. I was the right fit. I was in the right place. I was enough.

I was eager to share all this at the workshop, but as the time drew closer I began to fear no one would come. Although the pursuit of measuring up to others' expectations was a common theme

---

3. Brown, *Gifts of Imperfection*, 59–60. Brown borrows from the work of Dr. Kristin Neff, a researcher at the University of Texas, to explain what it means to be compassionate toward ourselves.

4. Brown, *Gifts of Imperfection*, 19.

when individual students talked confidentially with me, would any student acknowledge this publicly by attending the workshop? Ironically, my anxiety about no one showing up reflected my own feeling of "not being enough." But I need not have worried. The room was packed with students, much to my surprise and delight. I was grateful I had decided to offer the workshop, which turned out to be just what the attendees needed.

One student told me afterward, "You know, until today, no one had ever told me I could be kind to myself. And it had never occurred to me that I could tell myself that. I've always been told to try hard and if I didn't succeed, then I needed to try harder next time. In my mind, I heard the message that I wasn't trying hard enough and then I would beat myself up about it. I see now that it sets up a vicious cycle. No matter how hard I tried it felt like it was never enough. And the more I beat myself up about it, the more I felt like I wasn't enough. Starting today I'm going to be kind with myself. I am worth it. I am enough."

"Practicing courage, compassion, and connection in our daily lives is how we cultivate worthiness," says Brown.[5] It's how we learn to claim our own value and come to recognize we are enough.

5. Brown, *Gifts of Imperfection*, 7.

CHAPTER 5

The Photo Album

Practice of Nurture: Pay Attention to Your Inner Voice

ONE OF THE COUNSELORS from the Counseling Center on campus called to tell me about Musa, a Muslim student from West Africa. He was seeing her for issues of grief related to his parents' deaths. She wanted to refer him to me because he told her he felt like he was losing his faith. She thought I would be better equipped to address that particular concern with him.

I wondered, *What do I know about helping a Muslim find his faith?*

Then I reminded myself that I didn't need to be anxious about finding a solution for Musa; I could trust he had the answer within him. My role was to pay attention—and help him pay attention—to his inner voice.

Ever since the morning of Julie's memorial service, I had adopted this philosophy in my interactions with the students. Julie was an office manager for the Admissions Department and had known for more than a year that she was dying. She had asked me early on if

I would take care of her memorial service, and we had met several times to discuss her wishes.

I'd had plenty of time to prepare. And yet there I was, the morning of her service, with no idea what message I would share with her family, friends, co-workers, and students in just a few hours.

It wasn't that I hadn't thought about it. I'd thought about it quite a bit. Over the months, as Julie and I discussed her arrangements, I had reflected on what message she would want me to share, what message would honor her and reflect who she was and the hope that she had—the hope that we, too, could claim.

Whenever I thought about the message, I would be drawn toward the image on a card that was tacked on my office bulletin board: a beautiful orange tabby cat lounging on a windowsill. I dismissed trying to make a connection between the image and Julie. It seemed so random; she didn't even like cats. But even on the morning of her service, when I still didn't know what to say but knew I would have to figure it out pretty soon, my mind kept drifting back to that card.

I decided to stop resisting and go where my thoughts led.

Valerie, the supervisor of my hospital chaplaincy internship, gave me the card after my first shift working as a chaplain intern. It was the night shift, 7:00 pm until 7:00 am, and I had no idea what I was doing.

Four other interns and I had gone through a short orientation, but that had oriented us to the hospital, not to chaplaincy. Of course, we had been educated in chaplaincy—we had the book knowledge. But we had presumed we'd take baby steps in the *practice* of becoming chaplains, that perhaps Valerie would have us shadow her or another chaplain first or that we'd round with our fellow interns and figure out together what we were supposed to be doing.

That was not to be.

Valerie announced that we would each take a night shift, one of us for each day of the workweek, and that we would be the only chaplain on our shift. Each of us was terrified. We all felt woefully underprepared.

I remember Valerie coaching me before I started that first shift.

"The challenge with chaplaincy," she said in her soft, reliable voice, "is to resist the urge to do something. Chaplaincy is at its best when we can simply be with people, rather than trying to do something to fix the situation. So don't worry about what you'll do or what you'll say. Just be yourself. Be who you are. Be present."

Those words were not very helpful to me at the time.

As I anticipated, I was incredibly anxious that first shift, especially in my encounters with those whose loved ones had died moments before. I felt incompetent as I fought the urge, futile at times, to do something for them rather than simply be present with them. I discovered there was nothing simple about being present with people; it demanded my whole self to stay engaged.

The next morning, I received the card with the cat lounging on the windowsill from Valerie. On the inside of the card, she acknowledged the challenges I had faced the night before and thanked me for my work.

Her words and my experience felt completely incongruent with the lounging cat. At first, I thought she had just grabbed a card she had lying around, that the cat had nothing to do with the sentiments she'd written in the card. But then, as I gazed at that cat, I noticed a word at the bottom of the card, underneath the picture. It read, "Courage."

When I read that word, I knew this was not an accidental card Valerie had picked up; I knew she had chosen this card for me. I assumed she chose it to acknowledge the courage it took for me to plunge into my first chaplain shift alone, not having a clue what I was doing. But I had always been puzzled by the presence of the cat. I studied that card often over the years, trying to figure out how the picture of that lounging cat fit with the word *courage*. They just didn't go together.

I sat at my kitchen table the morning of Julie's memorial service, still reflecting on what message I would share at her service and still drawn to the image of the lounging cat and the word *courage*. I wanted to figure out how—or even if—any of it connected with Julie. My anxiety increased in proportion to my decreasing window of time.

As the minutes ticked by, I willed my furiously beating heart to slow down so I might calm down enough to center myself and be still and listen, really listen, to discover if there was a connection.

I closed my eyes and let my thoughts drift.

The cat lounging on the windowsill . . . courage . . . the night of my first chaplaincy shift . . . the life and dying and death of Julie . . . that lounging cat doing absolutely nothing on that windowsill . . . courage . . . I was supposed to be doing nothing on my chaplaincy shift . . .

And then came this notion: *It takes courage to do nothing.*

I opened my eyes with a start.

Could this have been what Valerie was trying to convey to me when she gave me the card? After all, on that first chaplaincy shift I was so tempted to *do something*. It was easier to do something for the people I encountered because it distracted me from having to be present to their pain.

Sometimes it *does* take courage to do nothing.

But what was the connection to Julie?

Julie had an aggressive form of breast cancer. Her sister had died from the same type of cancer that had metastasized throughout her body, and Julie didn't want to go through what her sister had suffered through trying to survive. So she made the decision not to fight her cancer. She chose not to undergo chemotherapy or other invasive treatments. She wanted to enjoy her quality of life in the time she had left.

It was a hard decision for Julie, not one she made lightly—and not one she made without a lot of pushback from her family and friends. But she stood firm in choosing the path she thought was best for her.

None of us would have thought to use the word *courage* to describe Julie's decision to do nothing. *Courage* was the word reserved for those who fight their cancers, not for those who don't.

Maybe that was why we couldn't see it.

We kept comparing Julie *not* fighting her cancer to those who *do* fight their cancer. And if those who fight their cancer are courageous and Julie was doing the opposite of fighting . . . well, then, what Julie was doing, though none of us would dare to say it, was cowardly. Logically speaking, that is.

We couldn't see that it required courage for Julie to listen to her own heart, her own inner voice, when it went against conventional wisdom and medical advice. It took courage for her to fight the urge to do what everyone was recommending she do. It took courage for her to stand up for what she believed was the right thing for her when others accused her of giving up. It took courage to do nothing, when everything and everyone was telling her to *do something*.

It took courage for Julie to stare death in the face and not try to outrun it. By choosing not to aggressively treat her cancer, she had to have the courage to see death for what it was, stripped free of the disguises it often hides behind. By choosing not to run from death, Julie had to have the courage to see it was not something she had to fear and avoid at all costs—even the cost of her quality of life.

I sat at my kitchen table, astonished there was actually a connection between Julie, the cat on the windowsill card, and my first chaplaincy shift.

Who would have thought?

I finally had my message for Julie's service, which was great. I should have been celebrating. Instead, I felt deflated. I couldn't stop thinking that I wished I'd said these words to her when she was still alive. I wished I'd paid attention to those flitting thoughts about the cat on the windowsill earlier, before she died.

I shared all of this at Julie's service. And as I stood behind the podium at the front of the sanctuary and shared the minute-by-minute replay of the angst I paddled through to find a connection point between Julie and the cat on the windowsill, I noticed people fussing in their seats and looking at their watches. I saw their eyes shifting to the left and the right in an oh-so-subtle way (but not subtle enough) to see if others were thinking the same thing they were. I knew what they were thinking. I could sense the growing impatience and tension in the room.

Finally, I couldn't stand it any longer.

I halted in the middle of my prepared message and blurted out, "I can sense that all of you are trying to figure out how any of this has anything to do with Julie. Well, I have to tell you, that's *exactly* what I was trying to figure out too!"

I was struck by the unintentional effect my outburst had on the people gathered. There was a collective sigh of relief. And then they seemed to lean forward to hear the rest, now that they'd been reassured I knew we were there for Julie and that there was some kind of point I wanted to bring home to them.

They became mesmerized as I related the connection I'd discovered between my story and Julie's story. And then, as I shared about Julie's courage, I saw recognition in their eyes. I observed some heads nodding confirmation. I saw wistful, even regretful, looks on people's faces. They identified themselves within the story. It was no longer my story; it had become *our* story.

It turned out this was a word they needed to hear that day. Some of them had been angry with Julie for not doing anything to save herself. Weeks after the service, several of her friends told me my message had helped them work through their resentment so they could honor her memory. They, too, wished they could have done this while she was still alive, that they could have respected her decision and recognized and affirmed the courage she possessed. But their feeling that she was a quitter had kept genuine conversation at bay. It had been hard for them to be present with her because they wanted to fix the situation; they wanted to *do something* to make her *do something* to fix the situation.

It made me wonder why I had kept ignoring the persistent thoughts about the cat on the windowsill that flooded my brain every time I thought about Julie's service.

Why had I not paid attention?

I guess because it didn't seem logical. But that's the way my inner voice down in my heart often works. It's trying to tell me something that the logical voice up in my head would dismiss. And there are the other logical voices up there, too, the ones I don't always recognize are not my own. Like my father's voice that says, "You're not good enough. Try harder." Or my mother's voice that says, "Your appearance could be improved upon." Or the church's voice that says, "You should be doing it this way."

I often mistake these voices for my own inner voice. But when I really pay attention, I can discern the difference.

I have discovered my inner voice is not one that uses *could* and *should* and *not good enough*. My inner voice is that authentic, genuine part of who I am that speaks truth into my life. It doesn't tear me down when it speaks the truth; it doesn't criticize. It's not out to harm me or others. So if I have thoughts of ill will, I do well to remember those thoughts come from somewhere else. My inner voice simply tries to get my attention so I might notice the truth in a way that I can hear it and embrace it for my own good, and for the good of others too.

The spiritual writer Macrina Wiederkehr calls it our *knowing place*. She writes, "Deep within your soul there is a *knowing place*, a sanctuary where gifts are nurtured. Enter that sacred space. Spend time there tending your gifts. There in the chapel of your heart you will become a gift to be given."[1]

My inner voice doesn't impose itself on me. It doesn't yell or whine or bribe or bargain. It's a small voice, and it can be easy for me to dismiss it in the cacophony of voices competing for attention in my head.

It is patient and persistent, though, like I saw with the cat card and Julie, so if I turn my attention toward it, tune out the distractions, quiet myself, and listen closely, then sometimes I can hear what it is saying. Often it offers me wisdom I'm not sure I would have found otherwise. When this happens, I'm reminded of a saying from the Psalms: "You desire truth in the inward being; therefore teach me wisdom in my secret heart."[2]

1. Wiederkehr, *Song of the Seed*, 113.
2. Ps 51:6.

༂༐

After what happened on that day of Julie's service, I began to pay more attention to my inner voice—and the inner voice of others. When students would talk to me about the hard things going on in their lives, I realized I didn't have to feel anxious about trying to come up with solutions that might help them fix their situations. I learned to trust they had the answers within themselves. I learned to trust that their inner voice would speak up at some point and that I could help that happen.

I practiced with them what I had learned to practice with myself: I paid attention to what they were saying, asked questions that helped them sift through the different voices that were a part of their story, and noticed connections. Then they often discerned which voice might be their own, their inner voice, the voice of their heart. It never ceased to amaze me how their inner voice could provide them with the wisdom they needed to live into their authentic selves, how it could help them recognize their options and make the choice that was congruent with who they were and who they wanted to be.

So on the day the counselor called me about Musa, the Muslim student who was losing his faith, and I felt anxious about my ability to help him, I reminded myself to calm down and pay attention—and to trust that Musa held the solution within him.

When Musa came to see me the next morning, he related that ever since his parents had died, he had not felt like going to the prayer room or to Friday service at the Islamic Center. He did not even feel like reading the Qur'an. But then he felt bad because he knew his parents would be displeased with him if they were still alive. They wanted him to be a good Muslim.

I thought about what it meant to be a good Christian. Was it the same thing? Making sure we pray and go to church on Sunday and read our Bible? Was this what I would tell a Christian student to do if he said he had lost his faith? These practices might be a sign of one's faith, but were they the way to finding faith that was lost?

I didn't really know where to begin with Musa, but it appeared that his loss of faith was related to the loss of his parents. So I started there.

"Musa, tell me about your parents," I said.

He told me how they had died. Six months ago, his mother succumbed to a chronic illness. More recently, his father was killed in a car accident.

I took this in, and then asked him, "What were your parents like before they died?"

His eyes brightened. He shared with me about his dad's kind heart and his mom's easygoing nature, and how they loved him and encouraged him to continue with his studies. Then he went still, frowning. His chin trembled a little.

I waited.

Finally he said, "I came to the States to study and earn a degree so I could go back to my country and make a good living and take care of my parents. Now that they are gone, I have no reason to keep studying. I have no reason to get a degree. I don't even have a reason to keep living. This is why I can't read my Qur'an or say my prayers or go to Friday services. What's the point?"

I acknowledged his loss with silence, letting his words settle into our space together.

Then I quietly asked, "What do you think was the point of participating in the practices of your faith when your parents were still alive? Was it only so they would be pleased with you, or did you do these practices for yourself too?"

He sat there pensively, eyes cast down. Then he replied, "I think it was a way to stay connected with God and with my religion and a way to connect with the other students here who share my religion. And it helped me feel connected with my parents back home, knowing they would be praying the same prayers I was. But now all it does is remind me that I can't connect with my mother and father anymore."

I thought about this. Then I said, "What if there is a different way to connect with your parents? I saw how your eyes lit up when you talked about what they were like when they were alive and how much they loved you. And it's apparent to me how much you love them. I think you were connecting with them in that way, through remembering the experiences you shared with them."

Musa sat there, seeming to ponder what I'd said.

I went on, "When you were talking about your parents, I was trying to picture what they looked like and where you all had lived together back in your country. And it made me wonder . . . do you have any photos of them on your phone?"

Marginally engaged, Musa fished his phone out of his pocket and began to scroll through his photos. He showed me one of his mom at their house, then one of his dad standing outside. He gradually became more motivated and looked for others. He showed me those and shared with me when they were taken and where they were located geographically.

Then, suddenly, he looked up at me. I could see the hope in his eyes and I heard it in his voice as he said, "I have a photo album back in my dorm room with pictures of my mom and dad. Would it be okay if I ran and got it and brought it back here to show you? I can be quick. Will you still be here?"

I promised him I would.

He left and returned about ten minutes later, breathing heavily. He said he ran the entire way. We sat down and he opened his photo album, and we went page by page, looking at the photos as I asked questions and Musa told the stories that surrounded each picture. It was a hallowed time, Musa connecting with his parents through his memories brought alive by the photo album. He remembered the good times with his parents; he remembered who they were in life, not just in death.

As we looked at the last picture and Musa closed the album, he glanced at his watch and said, "It's almost time for noonday prayer. I think I'll stop by the prayer room on my way out."

My eyebrows arched at this declaration, but he missed my questioning look, as he was already gathering his things and seemed eager to leave. Not feeling like I had offered any real guidance to him about his loss of faith, I asked if he would like to make another appointment with me. By this time he was at my office door, with one foot in the hallway, and he turned to say he would check back in with me in a week or so.

I really didn't think I would see him again.

It was close to a month later when he returned. He looked like a different person, his countenance relaxed and his voice strong.

"I am doing so much better," he said. "I am back to my prayers and attending Friday services and reading the Qur'an. I feel like I have purpose to my life now."

I was pleasantly surprised. "Musa, I'm so glad you're feeling better," I said. "You look great! It sounds like you're moving forward with your life. It sounds like you have a plan. Tell me about it."

He began talking excitedly. "I want to finish my studies here—get my degree. Then I want to return home and work to make peace between the Muslims and the Christians in my country. They fight a lot where I live, and I want to help them see that we might have a lot of differences in our religions, but as people we're not that different; we're not that different at all. I want to tell them about the Christian I met here who sat and looked at my photo album with me and helped me reconnect with my faith."

I sat there speechless, trying to piece together what he was saying, trying to rewind the video in my mind of our time together, trying to sort out just when it was that I helped him reconnect with his faith. But I couldn't locate it.

Eventually, as he was looking at me expectantly, I came back to the present and said, "Wow, that sounds like quite a plan! I'm so happy for you, Musa."

As he beamed, I ventured to say, "I remember our time of looking at your photo album and how it helped you reconnect with your parents. But how did our time together help you reconnect with your faith?"

He said, "It was the feeling I got from showing you the photo album, the feeling that someone cared about me. It helped me remember God cares about me too. I want to help the Muslims and the Christians in my country know that we can care about each other, even though we have different beliefs. I want them to know God cares about all of us, not just those who believe like we do."

I was amazed at how Musa had been able to connect with his inner voice and where it eventually led him. It brought home to me the words of Macrina Wiederkehr. He had found his knowing place. There in the chapel of his heart he had become a gift to be given.

CHAPTER 6

Stuck in the Stadium

Practice of Nurture: Remember Our Shared Humanity

"Does the Bible say it's okay for husbands to hit wives?" asked Rachel, a student who had just stepped into my office.

I invited her in, and we sat down together as I considered her question. Somehow I didn't think it was theology she really wanted to talk about. I chose my words carefully.

"No, the Bible does not say that," I said. "In fact, it says just the opposite—that husbands and wives should be gentle with each other. Did someone tell you that it's okay?"

Rachel hesitated, then replied, "My boyfriend said the Bible says it's okay to hit."

"Is your boyfriend hitting you?" I asked.

Rachel looked down, nodded slightly, then whispered to the floor, "I don't want to get him in any trouble."

I leaned forward and gently probed. "Are you okay with him hitting you?"

Her head jerked up, and she looked at me with tears in her eyes. "No! I want it to stop," she emphatically proclaimed. Then more quietly, she repeated, "I just don't want to get him in trouble."

"Do you want to get out of your relationship with him?" I asked.

Rachel nodded. "That's why I came here today, but now I'm not so sure. It's so complicated. We've been dating for about a year now, and we recently moved in together. He's a student here, too. I don't want him to get kicked out of school because of me. I just don't know how to leave him. The hitting wasn't really that bad in the beginning, but it has steadily gotten worse, and I just don't want to live like this anymore."

I asked if she would be okay with my calling the campus Counseling Center to see if we could go over there together and talk to one of the counselors about different options available to her. She reluctantly agreed, and when I phoned the director of the center, she invited us to come right over, as I knew she would.

Rachel and I walked together across the campus and entered the Counseling Center, where I waited with her until one of the counselors called her back. I knew the counselors would help connect her with the Domestic Abuse Council in town, and together they would have the resources that would empower Rachel to get out of this abusive relationship.

It wasn't until I got back to my office that I remembered the article I had submitted the day before to the campus newspaper for the next week's edition.

Oh no.

The article was about encouraging students to stick with things when they get hard rather than taking the easy way out. I didn't want Rachel reading that, thinking she should stick it out with her boyfriend. I deliberated whether I had time to tweak the article and send the paper a revision or tell them to withhold it from publication. I looked up what I had written and read through it with Rachel's situation in mind.

The story was about a recent weekend visiting Wilson at Auburn and attending a football game. Walking toward the stadium on the afternoon of the game, dark clouds rolled in suddenly, thunder rumbled like a freight train, and lightning flashed all around us. We ran the rest of the way, but we couldn't beat the rain and by the time we reached the stadium gates we were drenched.

We weren't allowed to go to our seats until the lightning passed and then we still had to wait for the delayed game to start. But we didn't care. We were excited to be there, anticipating a good game, and we weren't going to let the weather dampen our spirits.

But then, the game started. In their first possession, the other team scored a touchdown. Then, in their second possession, they scored another touchdown. I looked up at the game clock and exactly four minutes and forty-one seconds had gone by. I was wet and cold and had patiently waited over an hour for the game to start only to look forward to the next three or four hours of the other team pummeling our team.

It was then I knew I shouldn't have come. I should have told Wilson no that morning when we heard the forecast, or at least by the time we got to campus and saw the approaching storm. I should have talked him into leaving after the storm passed, after we were packed in like sardines under the stadium with all the smells from so many bodies wafting through the stale air. I remember thinking that maybe, just maybe I could talk him into leaving after the awful start to the game. But when I looked over at him, he didn't look like he was going to budge from his seat.

I was stuck.

I hate that feeling; the way it feels when I can't go back but I can't move forward either. I miserably settled in for the long haul.

Then, just about the time I had resigned myself to my stuckness, things began to change. Auburn made a field goal. Then they made a touchdown. Things were beginning to look up and it only got better from there. The second half was incredible, Auburn making five interceptions and three more touchdowns to win the game. It turned out to be one of the best times I ever had at a football game. As we headed home, exhausted yet exuberant, I thought back to the beginning of the game and what I would have missed if I had talked Wilson into leaving.

As I read the article with Rachel in mind, it was the last paragraph that really stood out to me:

I hate that feeling of being stuck, and I am a big fan of getting unstuck. Yet, as I looked back on that game, I could not help but think that maybe I can be a little too quick to want to get myself unstuck. When I tend to focus on the stuck-ness, I can't even imagine the possibilities that might present themselves if I just wait and see.

I had written the article because I thought my football game experience was a cute little story that might encourage students to slow down and think through their knee-jerk reactions when they wanted to quit something before they'd given it a chance. I had been thinking about things like courses and roommates, maybe a student organization they'd joined but then didn't want to commit to. I had not been thinking about the harder things in life, like harmful relationships or domestic violence. I had not been thinking about the kinds of things we don't generally associate with college students. I should have known better, though. I knew the students were not immune to the harsher realities of life. I knew the saying "The college years are the best years of your life" was not true for many of them.

I didn't want Rachel reading this article, thinking she should stay in a harmful relationship and imagining the possibility that it might get better. I didn't want anyone reading the article to think that. These kinds of relationships do not get better; they only get worse.

I revised the last paragraph of the article by inserting the following: *Often times, it is a very good thing to get unstuck (a necessity if stuck in a harmful situation). But, other times, it just might be worthwhile to wait and see.*

I felt better about that and emailed the new version to the newspaper office.

Several weeks later, my administrative coordinator Esther and I were sitting in her office chatting when we thought we heard someone crying. I got up and looked out into the hallway but didn't see anyone.

I tucked my head back in her door. "I think it's coming from one of the prayer rooms. I'll go check."

I looked through the little window in the door to the Catholic prayer room but didn't see anyone. Then I walked across the hall to the Jewish prayer room and peered in that door window. There sat a student who looked visibly upset.

I opened the door and stepped in, my hand still on the doorknob. "Hi," I said. "I'm Melynne, the chaplain. Would you like to talk?"

I wasn't prepared for what happened next.

The student jumped up, took a step toward me and shrieked, "Are you the chaplain that told my girlfriend to break up with me?!"

His rage was so intense that I felt physically threatened, although he had not raised his hand toward me. I reminded myself that I was the chaplain and he obviously needed someone to talk to.

Keeping my hand on the knob of the open door, I suggested, "Why don't we sit down and talk?"

He took another step toward me and continued his wrath. "I don't want to sit down and I don't want to talk! I just want to know if you're the chaplain who told my girlfriend to break up with me!"

I stood my ground and declared in a calm and surprisingly strong voice that belied the inner quaking I felt, "We can sit down and talk about what is concerning you; however, if you continue to yell at me, then I will have to ask you to leave the premises."

He slumped back into his chair, and his anger seemed to slump with him as he began to weep, tears rolling down his anguished face and merging with the mucus running from his nose. He smeared it into a blubbery mess when he tried to stem the flow from his nose with the back of his hand.

I took that opportunity to let him know I was going to grab some tissues for him and that I would be right back. He nodded as he dropped his head, which only exacerbated his need.

Esther's office was just outside the prayer rooms, and I slipped in there and quietly asked her to call Campus Safety. Always efficient, even in a crisis, she had them on the phone before I could clarify that I was safe and thought I would continue to be safe but that if Campus Safety had a patrol officer available who could come over and hang out on standby I would feel better about going back to talk with this student. She relayed the message as I grabbed a box of tissues off her desk and headed back into the prayer room, closing the door behind me for privacy.

I handed the young man the tissues and asked, "What is your name?"

"Mike." He blew his nose and swiped at his face with the tissues.

"Mike, can you tell me what's going on?"

"My girlfriend left me. She wrote a goodbye note, and in it she said she came here and talked to a chaplain who told her the Bible says hitting is not okay. Why would you tell her that?"

I took a deep breath to gather my thoughts and discern how to proceed. "Mike, I cannot disclose to you who comes to see me. But what I can tell you is that if anyone were to ask me if the Bible says hitting is okay, I would tell them no, the Bible does not say hitting is okay."

Mike wiped the tears from his face, blew his nose again, and sat up a little straighter. Then he dove into a dissertation about why he was convinced it was biblically appropriate to hit those you love when the occasion called for it.

I sat there staring at him, speechless. I could feel the ire rising in me. I wanted to give him a lesson in how to read and interpret the Bible. I wanted to tell him specific verses were never meant to be taken out of context, that whatever he read needed to be read in light of the whole. I wanted to painstakingly and patronizingly teach him how to do it. I wanted to tell him that if he read something in the Bible that he interpreted in a way that justified causing harm to others, then he had misinterpreted the Bible.

I was so pumped up to deliver my exhortation; I was burning to say those things to him. But I caught myself. Now was not the time to get bogged down in a theological debate about this topic. We had other hurdles to tackle.

I collected my self-control and asked him, "Have you been hitting someone you love?"

Mike slumped again. His tears threatened and his voice quivered as he mournfully responded, "No . . . not anymore, because she's gone. She's left. She moved out. And she left school too. I don't know where she went. She was the love of my life, and now I'm never going to see her again."

The tears fell unchecked as sobs heaved into a torrent of loud—and long—lament.

Mike had not used his girlfriend's name (and Rachel had never mentioned her boyfriend's name), so I didn't know if he was referring to Rachel. She wasn't the only student who had visited me in the same predicament, asking questions about the Bible and abuse. And he wasn't the only student who had visited me in his predicament either. Even so, I offered up a silent prayer of gratitude that his girlfriend had left the relationship and that she was safe. Then I brought my attention back to Mike.

What was I going to do with him?

I wanted to rationalize that he was not really looking for compassion and that he certainly didn't deserve it. What kind of person would hit someone they supposedly loved?

That was when I finally recognized in myself an aversion to Mike.

Despite my repugnance, I could sense his lament reaching somewhere deep in my spirit. It prompted me to remember he was a human being, just like me. As I grudgingly offered up my assent to this sacred truth, I discovered myself leaning in and inquiring, "Mike, has there ever been anyone in your life who has hit you?"

For the next hour, Mike shared with me stories from his childhood. He'd grown up in an abusive home, and we traced the pattern of behavior that was handed down to him and that he had perpetuated, a cycle of violence seemingly with no end.

Mike was stuck.

It brought to mind again my article about being stuck in the stadium. I had visions of students stuck in unhealthy behaviors, saying to themselves, "It just might be worthwhile to wait and see if anything improves." I knew there was nothing about an unhealthy pattern of behavior that a "wait and see" approach would rectify.

I sighed. I should have never written that article. I should have never revised and resubmitted it. I should have never let it be published.

But then I remembered some of the other words I'd written in it. Words like, *When I tend to focus on the stuck-ness, I can't even imagine the possibilities that might present themselves.*

And that's when I gently redirected Mike from our focus on the cycle of violence to which he was bound, and toward what it might look like for him to be unshackled from it. We imagined together what the process of unlearning this behavior could look like. We talked about the hard work it would require, the resources and the therapy and the resolve. And we talked about the hope— hope that would need to be sustained over the long haul; hope that healing might eventually open up a space within him where he could receive love and offer love in life-nurturing ways.

As our time together came to a close, Mike promised he would follow up with a counselor he had seen the week before, after his girlfriend had left him. As I stood up to leave, he said he wanted to stay in the prayer room a while longer and collect his thoughts. I nodded and said goodbye.

I closed the door behind me and went to check in with Esther. As I crossed the threshold of her office, I saw a Campus Safety officer sitting in a chair opposite her desk. I stopped in my tracks, my hand flying to my mouth in surprise. With all that had transpired with Mike, I had forgotten about requesting the officer. I looked at my watch, wondering how long I had kept him here.

"Thank you so much for coming," I said. "I'm so sorry I've kept you here so long. I wasn't even thinking . . ."

"No need to apologize. It was no problem at all," he replied. "That's what we're here for. It's a slow day anyway. And I've enjoyed catching up with Esther. I wanted to wait until you came out to make sure you were okay." He gave me a questioning look.

"Oh, yes, I'm fine," I assured them both. "It went so much smoother than I could have thought it would at the outset. But thank you again for showing up and hanging out here."

I made my way back to my office, the encounter with Mike forefront in my thoughts. It felt like our shared humanity was the only thing I could hang on to in that space between us. Remarkably, it had been enough to foster a connection.

CHAPTER 7

Second Chances

Practice of Nurture: Show Kindness

CHRIS, A THIRD-YEAR STUDENT, was in a motorcycle accident that landed him in the Intensive Care Unit of our local hospital. He was in a coma. When I went to check on him, I found the ICU waiting room filled with his family and friends.

I introduced myself as the chaplain, and a woman who turned out to be Chris's mother clasped her hands together and exclaimed, "Oh, good! I'm so glad you're here! Maybe you'll have some insight on why God allowed this to happen to my son. There must be some reason, some sin that he, or maybe someone else in our family, committed that has caused him to lose favor in God's sight."

I looked at her in astonishment. "You think God caused this to happen to Chris? It was an accident. God doesn't cause these things to happen," I said in a reassuring voice.

I thought this would bring her some comfort.

"Oh, yes, he does!" she countered. "God caused King David's baby to die because he committed adultery with Bathsheba!"[1]

I was doubly astonished and at a loss for words. I considered telling her that when we look at the Bible holistically and interpret individual stories in light of the whole, we get a clearer picture of

---

1. She was referring to the story found in 2 Sam 11:1—12:25.

God's character. We're able to see God is not a punishing God but rather a compassionate God who comes right alongside us in the muck that life brings us, who offers comfort and strength and hope and peace as we deal with things like our children laying in ICU, holding on to life by a thread.

But why should I try and refute her? She seemed determined about her belief. And I was reminded, once again, that my role as chaplain was not to challenge her beliefs or give her a lesson in scriptural interpretation. My role was to support her in ways that brought her comfort and strength and peace and hope. If her beliefs did that for her, then my role was to support her in that.

It was frustrating, though. It was hard for me to grasp how her belief that God caused this to happen to her son would bring her any comfort or peace.

Finally, I gathered my wits about me, smiled tightly, and responded, "Let's just hope for the best."

A few days later, one of the campus ministers who led a Christian group on campus came by the hospital and asked Chris's mom if she'd like for him to hold a prayer service for Chris in the hospital chapel. She said yes, so he scheduled it for the next day, and everyone got the word out about it.

I was leery about the service because I had a hunch this campus minister, like Chris's mother, believed God caused Chris's accident and would spout his claims to all the students who attended. I vacillated back and forth about whether to even attend, but in the end I decided to go. As I slipped in late, I noticed the intimate chapel was almost full with Chris's friends. Then I spotted his mother; she appeared captivated by what the campus minister was saying.

I listened to him speak about how God always has a plan and that Chris's accident was all part of this grander plan.

Just as I thought.

"We can't see it now," he proclaimed, "but one day we will understand why this happened. We just have to have hope and keep a good attitude that it will all work out. But if it doesn't, we're still called to rejoice that this is a piece of God's plan."

I felt like I should speak up, like I should say something about how there are other ways of looking at why bad things happen, other ways of looking at who God is and how God is active in the world.

Then I looked over at Chris's mom and was taken aback. She was beaming. She looked radiant. She actually looked like she was at peace. I had to admit to myself that the campus minister's words seemed to bring her comfort.

I worried about all the students hearing his words, though. Would this message bring them harm? I didn't want them assuming this was the only way to view God. But I didn't want to be rude and contradict the campus minister, especially with the way Chris's mom was responding to it.

I squirmed in my seat.

I thought maybe I should get up and leave, slip out early the same way I slipped in late. But that would be rude too. I resigned myself to keeping my mouth shut and waiting it out until it was over.

At the end of the service, when we got up to leave, I noticed a student who looked familiar, but I couldn't place him. I'd not seen him with the other groups of students who had been hanging out together in the ICU waiting room over the last few days.

I walked down the hospital corridor, racking my brain as to where I had seen him before, when all of a sudden it hit me. He was the student in the car accident last year. His name was Darien, if I remembered correctly.

The summer before, there had been a car accident on a curvy river road in a neighboring town that involved two of our students. The passenger died at the scene. The driver of the car, who had lost control going around one of the bends in the road, was this student, Darien. He'd had minor injuries, mostly bruises and scratches.

The parents of the deceased student, whose name was Emily, asked if we would hold a memorial service for their daughter once we resumed classes in the fall. And so we did. Emily's parents traveled from their home in Illinois to be there for it, and I spent the morning prior to the service with them.

They shared with me how grief had taken a toll on them and their family. They also shared the myriad of feelings they felt about the student who had driven the car. They had never met him but knew he had been a good friend of their daughter's. They shared with me the anger they had felt toward him but also that they had come to a place in their hearts where they wanted to forgive him. They asked if I would arrange for them to meet with Darien after the service.

I was somewhat hesitant about their request. Who knew what these parents might feel once they saw Darien face-to-face? I didn't want him to be subjected to an angry outburst from one, or both, of Emily's parents. But I also thought Darien should know about their request and make his own informed decision. So I told the parents I would contact him.

When I did, Darien said that he, too, wanted to meet with them, so I made the arrangements for all of us to meet after Emily's memorial service. I had no idea what to expect.

When Emily's parents saw Darien for the first time, they not only saw the person who drove the car that killed their daughter; they also saw a young man devastated by what happened and full of remorse. In the midst of their own deep grief, they were able to show compassion toward Darien.

They asked him how he had been doing since the accident, and they listened intently as he shared how it had been hard to get his life back together and on track. They acknowledged that not only was he dealing with the effects of the accident, but also that he had lost one of his good friends. They told him they did not want him to be consumed by this tragedy but to work through his grief, pick up the pieces of his life, and move forward. Otherwise, there would be two tragedies. They told Darien they did not hold Emily's death against him and that they wanted him not to hold it against himself. I remember he thanked them for being so kind to him.

That was the last I had seen of Darien until the prayer service for Chris.

I wondered what he was thinking after hearing the minister's words about God's "grand plan." I regretted that I had not spoken up at the service, that I had not offered up another way to look at why bad things happen and how God responds.

I hurried back to the hospital chapel to see if Darien was still hanging around, but he had already left.

I went back to the hospital a few days later to check on Chris, who was still in a coma in ICU. On the way down the hall, I popped my head into the ICU waiting room and was surprised to see only one person in there; it had been so full of Chris's friends and family the previous times I had come by. I was even more surprised when I realized the one person sitting there was Darien.

I walked over to where he was sitting. "Hi Darien, I'm Melynne," I said. "I'm not sure if you remember me. I'm the chaplain from Emily's memorial service last year."

He looked up at me and nodded. "I remember you."

I sat down in a chair next to his and said, "I've been thinking a lot about you the past couple of days, ever since I noticed you at Chris's prayer service. I'd not realized you and he are friends. How are you doing with all this?"

"I'm doing okay," he responded in a noncommittal voice.

I waited.

He paused, then added, "Well, not exactly okay."

I waited some more.

He took a deep breath, rubbed his hands over his face, and then said, "It's hard, you know, with Chris's accident coming less than a year after Emily's death. Chris is a good friend of mine, too, just like Emily was."

I acknowledged this with a small nod and said, "That is hard. You've had a lot to deal with."

He sat there with his head bowed.

I sat back a little in my chair to give him some space and thought about how I might respond. Finally, I asked, "Darien, do you remember what Emily's parents said to you when we met with them after her service?"

He looked at me, then stared up at the ceiling, his jaw muscles working. "Yeah, I remember. They wanted me to move on with my life, not to let Emily's death get me bogged down."

"How has that been going for you?"

His eyes found mine, and he said, "Well, to be honest, it's been really hard."

He looked away again, and I wasn't sure if he would elaborate, but then the words tumbled out.

"And now this with Chris isn't helping," he said. "And then to hear that guy talk about how Chris's accident is all part of God's big plan—I don't get it. If Chris's accident is part of God's plan, then I guess that would mean my accident and Emily's death are part of God's plan too. But I don't buy that. I don't believe God wanted Emily to die and me to live. I don't believe God wants Chris to die, either. And if God is like that, then I don't even want to believe in God. Why do people even say things like that?" He hung his head, spent.

I wondered if it was a rhetorical question or if he was looking for an answer. I thought about Chris's mother and her blissful response to the prayer service. I decided to respond.

"I'm thinking perhaps people say things like that—and believe things like that—because it helps them make some sense out of something that doesn't make any sense. Maybe it helps them feel like they have some control to believe that God is in control of everything. Maybe it gives them some comfort to believe their loved one might be part of God's larger purposes."

Darien leaned toward me and asked, "Do *you* believe that stuff that guy said?"

I paused to consider whether to share my beliefs with Darien, remembering it was not my role to convince him to believe like I do. But I also remembered my role was to support him in whatever ways would bring him comfort and peace and hope.

Finally, I replied, "No, I don't believe that. I don't believe God causes these accidents to happen or that they're part of a bigger plan for humanity. But I do believe God is with us and that God wants to bring good out of the bad things that happen to us. I'm thinking about what Emily's parents said to you last year. They wanted you to be able to move forward with your life. I think they said that because they knew it would be redemptive, both for you *and* for them."

"Redemptive? What do you mean by that?"

"To me, redemption means to bring something good out of something bad that happens," I said. "Rather than staying focused on the question, 'Why did this happen?' it's about asking the question, 'How can I bring good out of it?' Redemption isn't fixated on the past; it's future-oriented, looking for and working toward bringing future good out of past tragedy. When something is redeemed, it brings new value, new meaning to our lives and often to the lives of others."

Darien had a puzzled, doubtful, even suspicious look on his face. Finally, he said, "So, if I can live a meaningful life and not let the car accident derail that, then it will redeem Emily's death? I guess I just don't get it. Nothing is going to make Emily's death less of a tragedy."

I agreed with him, nodding my head and saying, "That's true. Redemption is not about trying to deny or minimize what happened. Redemption acknowledges the enormity of the loss and wants us to grieve all that we've lost. And redemption grieves with us. And then, once we've worked through our grief—well, sometimes *even as* we are working through our grief—redemption asks, 'How, then, shall we move forward?'"

I could tell Darien was thinking about this. His head was cocked as he looked off into the distance of the room, trying to sort out what I was saying.

I continued. "Do you carry this tragedy around on your back the rest of your life, burdened down with guilt, as a means to atone for what happened? It won't bring Emily back, and it probably won't help you feel less guilty, either, because you'll be constantly reminded of it."

I saw a flicker of recognition in Darien's eyes.

I went on. "You know, we tend to think of atonement as some price we have to pay, some penance we have to do. But what if atonement is really about redeeming what was lost by seeking to bring good out of it?"

Darien didn't respond right away, and I sat there waiting, nothing breaking the silence except the ticking of the oversized industrial clock on the wall. Then in a small voice that sounded like a plea he asked, "But how do I do that?"

I answered his question with a question. "What if you ask yourself questions like, 'How might I live my life in a way that best honors Emily's memory? How might I live in a way that best embodies Emily's spirit? How might I live in a way that honors Emily's parents?' These are future-oriented questions, redemption-oriented questions. They focus on how you can bring future good out of the bad that has happened. This is what I believe God does when tragedy happens; God works with us to empower us to bring good out of it."

Darien sat there with his head down, elbows on his knees. I could tell he was in deep thought.

And I wondered if I had said too much, given him an earful of my own beliefs.

But then he looked up at me and said, "You know, I don't think I've been redeeming anything. I've been carrying this burden of guilt around with me, and like you say, it makes it really hard to try to move on with my life. I *want* to be future-oriented, but I feel like I have to bring the guilt along with me. It *does* feel like it's the price I'm supposed to pay because Emily died and I lived. How do I just shake that off?"

I nodded my head, acknowledging his dilemma with silence. We sat there in that empty space created by our lack of words yet filled with the enormity of Darien's question. I watched the second hand make a complete rotation around the face of the clock. And then another.

Eventually, I said, "Darien, Emily's parents have forgiven you. Have you forgiven yourself?"

He looked at me searchingly, then responded, "Well, I'm not sure. I'm not even sure if I know how to do that. I guess it feels like I would just be letting myself off the hook, so to speak."

I asked him, "Do you remember how Emily's parents treated you, how they assured you that they forgave you, that they didn't hold Emily's death against you?"

"Yeah . . . yeah, I do. It was really cool." He sighed with a wistful look on his face.

I asked, "Can you describe what that was like for you?"

"Well, I felt like they really saw me. I felt like they saw me as a real person and not just the guy who was driving the car that killed their daughter. They saw me as their daughter's good friend. They could see that I felt some of the same sadness they were feeling. It was like they had put themselves in my shoes and tried to imagine what that must feel like. They were so incredibly kind to me." Darien's eyes welled up.

I nodded my head. "Yes. Yes, they were. Do you think you could be that way with yourself?"

"What do you mean?"

"Could you be kind with yourself? Could you put yourself in your own shoes and see yourself as more than just the driver of the car that killed Emily? Could you really look at what you've been through with the grief of losing your good friend? Could you make the choice not to hold this against yourself? When you describe how Emily's parents forgave you, how incredibly kind they were with you, that's the same path to forgiving yourself."

Darien nodded his head and was wiping the tears from his eyes when a group of Chris's friends burst into the waiting room, talking over one another in their excitement. Chris had woken up from his coma. It looked like he was going to be okay.

CHAPTER 8

Leah's Legacy

Practice of Nurture: Suspend Judgment

SOME COLLEGE STUDENTS DON'T leave a note behind before they die by suicide. Others do. These notes are usually short, hand-written missives, often scrawled on a scrap of paper. And then there was Leah, a twenty-three-year-old graduate student, who left a three-page, single-spaced, typed letter detailing exactly why she was choosing to end her own life. She had written an open letter to the attendees of her funeral to explain her views on why suicide should be seen as acceptable for those who decide their life is no longer worth living.

When her family met with me to discuss arrangements for a funeral service on campus, they told me about their daughter's request to have her letter read at her funeral. I wanted to honor Leah, yet the last thing I wanted was for our students to hear that suicide is a viable alternative when life no longer seems worthwhile. I knew the statistics about suicide and college students.[1] And I knew some of the stories that made up those statistics.

1. For more information see afsp.org (American Foundation for Suicide Prevention).

74

Every time one of our students died, I made the phone call to the family on behalf of the university to offer our condolences. All of these calls were hard, but the hardest one was the call I made to the mother in Seattle—or it may have been San Francisco. I just remember it felt like she was so far away, on the shores of a different ocean, even though we shared the same country.

Her daughter, Alicia, a second-semester freshman, had died by suicide. The mother's unimaginable grief was expressed in the guise of anger toward me, whom she considered to be the embodiment of the institution.

She wanted to know why no one knew her child was suicidal. How could no one know? Her professors didn't know; her friends didn't know; not even her roommates suspected anything amiss with her. And, she added, how could *she* have known, being so far away? She said that whenever Alicia called, she always told her everything was going well. She said she believed her. She said she had no reason not to believe her. She said she had entrusted her child to us and we had failed her.

We had failed her.

I had heard those words before. During Wilson's freshman year at college, a student who lived across the hall from him in his dorm, a first-year coed, was abducted from the campus library parking lot and later found dead outside of town. I still remember the words of the college president as he spoke to the community. He said, "Parents bring their children to our college, and they entrust their children to us. And it is our responsibility to ensure our campus is safe and secure for their children. We have let these parents down. We have failed them."

Those of us who work on college campuses may have different roles, but at the core of what we do, whether we're a chaplain or a custodian or a college president, is ensure the wellbeing of our students. We want to keep them safe—physically, emotionally, spiritually—so they are freed up to reach their full potential.

We had failed Alicia. We had failed Alicia's mother.

I could feel her anguish, even through the wispy telephone connection. I felt it right down to the marrow of my bones. And I had no word for her. No word of comfort, and certainly no word of defense. All I could do was acknowledge her words, absorb them as they came barreling down the telephone line, bearing witness to her grief by allowing her words to be borne upon me.

I used to think I carried the grief of others like a shawl over my shoulders. But after that phone call to Alicia's mother, I discovered grief is not something that can be contained and carried like a bag of groceries. Grief is more like a vapor; it seeps into me, into my muscles, my blood, my bones, my breath, the sinews of my inner being. I can't shake it off the way I might throw off a shawl. I can't lay it down the way I might set down a sack of potatoes. Sometimes I'm not even sure where in my body the grief has already meandered off to, where it has already settled in and made a home for itself. All I know is that I feel heavier than I did before.

After I finished that phone call, my head dropped into my hands and I wept. I wept for this mother and for her child, for the way Alicia had slipped through our safety net, for the way we had no way of knowing she was suicidal, and for the way we had failed her by having no way of knowing.

At the same time, I knew I was weeping for myself and for my own children, all three now away at colleges scattered across three states. Whenever one of them called home, they told me everything was going well. And I believed them. Would there be a reason not to believe them? How would I know? How would any of us know?

I routinely visited our students who ended up in one or another of the psychiatric units in our community. I remember the first time I went to check on one of these students who had been admitted to the psych unit at our local hospital after he attempted suicide. I felt unprepared, which made me anxious, which made me fearful, which eventually found expression in judgmental contemplations.

I stood outside a locked door that had a sign on it that read "Do Not Enter. Call First. Use Wall Phone." I picked up the receiver with the black curly cord connecting it to the old-fashioned rotary phone hanging on the wall. I dialed the number.

What would I say? I didn't even know this student.

"Hello, Psych Unit," said the voice on the other end of the line.

"Hello," said a shrill voice I didn't recognize as my own.

I cleared my throat, then continued, each of my sentences ending with a high-pitched squeal that gave the impression I was asking questions instead of making declarations. "This is Reverend Rust? The chaplain from the college? I understand we have a student admitted to your unit, and, uh, I would like to visit him? If that's okay?"

"Patient's name?" came the disembodied voice.

I gave the student's name as I worked to bring my voice back into a range that sounded professional and confident.

"I'll have to check with him and see if he would like a visit," the voice answered. "What did you say your name was again?"

My voice, of its own volition, rose back up. "Well, you see, the thing is . . . he doesn't know me. Just tell him I'm the chaplain from the college."

She put me on hold, and after I listened to three cycles of mundane music, she came back on the line and said, "Yes, he says he would like a visit. I will buzz you through."

After I hung up the phone, I let out a long sigh. This was when I acknowledged to myself that I had been hoping he would say no. I didn't want to have to visit a psychiatric patient who resided behind locked doors. Who knew what kind of craziness I might find?

I walked through the door and down the corridor to the Nurses Station. The clerk instructed me to put my purse in a locker and lock it. Then she introduced me to an orderly, who unlocked a door and motioned me through. He escorted me down a long hallway, through another locked door, and down another hallway, his sundry of keys jangling against his ample hips.

I took deep breaths as we walked, trying to get my heartbeat down to a manageable level. We walked some more, and then he unlocked one final door, and there in front of me was my student, sitting in a chair and looking a little disheveled.

The orderly said, "I'll leave you two alone so you have some privacy. When you're finished, buzz this button on the wall here, and I'll come back to get you."

Alone? In the bowels of the hospital's psych ward with someone who might be crazy?

I watched the orderly walk through the doorway and close the door. I could hear him on the other side locking it, locking us in. I took one more deep breath, turned around, and smiled tentatively at my student.

He smiled back at me.

This is when I remembered I was wearing my cross necklace. *Oh dear.*

I knew from the information I received from his friends and the Dean of Students Office that this student, Nathan, was twenty years old, a sophomore majoring in engineering. He was an international student from London. And he was Jewish.

For the most part, I had stopped wearing my religious jewelry. I didn't want it to be a barrier in my interactions with students from other faith traditions. Some of my colleagues said I was denying my faith by doing this, but I saw it as bearing witness to the hospitality of God, a way to embody a welcoming spirit.

Why did I wear my cross necklace today, of all days?

I sat down across from Nathan and tried to forget about my necklace. From his dazed expression, I wasn't sure he was even aware of what I was wearing.

My thoughts raced. *Where do I begin? What is his cognitive level? Is he in la-la land, or is he dwelling in reality? Why does the staff in this unit insist on keeping everything so hush-hush that I don't even know if I am safe sitting here alone with him? Surely I'm safe, or they wouldn't have left me alone with him. Surely. But what if I say something that sends him over the edge? What if my cross necklace sends him over the edge? Why am I even here? Where do I begin?*

"Nathan, my name is Melynne, and I'm the chaplain over at the college," I finally said. "I just wanted to come by and say hello and see how you are doing."

Nathan nodded and smiled some more.

"I've talked to some of your friends back on campus," I continued, "and they said to tell you hello."

Nathan's body began to rock ever so slowly, forward toward me, then back again; forward, then back. I found myself mimicking his motion, just a slight movement forward, then back again. It soothed me and calmed my nerves a bit. Maybe it was doing the same for him.

I looked at him and tried to put myself in his place. I had never been a patient in a mental health unit, but I had a few episodes when I felt like I lost touch with reality. I remembered feeling very afraid, somehow knowing deep within me that something had gone askew but not knowing what it was or how to make it right again. I remembered feeling so lonely, isolated by my break with reality.

"Nathan, your friends wanted you to know that they are thinking of you," I said. "You are not alone."

Nathan continued to rock, his rhythmic movement setting a cadence. The two of us rocked in connected silence. Nathan's face looked placid. Calm. Maybe even peaceful. I wondered if mine did too.

It was then that I took stock of myself. My heartbeat had returned to normal. I was no longer afraid.

We are not alone.

I wasn't sure how much time passed in this way, but eventually I told Nathan it was time for me to go. I asked him if he would like for me to come back for another visit.

He nodded affirmatively and smiled at me.

Unfortunately, another visit never happened. I went back the next day and went through the ritual outside the locked door to the Psych Unit. I was told Nathan had taken a turn for the worse and could no longer receive visitors. The voice would not give me any more information than that.

"But I promised him I would come back and visit," I pleaded.

The voice told me she would let him know, but she didn't think he would remember anyway. I wasn't allowed to see him the rest of his stay. When he was discharged, he went directly to his family's home in England accompanied by his father, who had flown in to get him. I wondered if Nathan would ever return to our college.

Months later, a week before classes started for the new semester, a young man and his parents walked into the chapel. He came up to me with a big smile on his face, like he knew me, but I didn't recognize him. Then I looked closer and asked, "Nathan? Is that you?"

He exclaimed, "It's me! It's me! Don't I look great?!"

And he did. He looked like a completely different person. He looked healthy and vibrant, even passionate.

Before I could respond, he continued enthusiastically, "I wanted to come and thank you for visiting me when I was in the hospital. I wanted my parents to meet you. I told them about you."

After the introductions were made, the three of them shared with me about Nathan's stay in the Psych Unit, the diagnosis of bipolar disorder, the treatment he received, the medication he was on, and how well he was doing now, ready to resume his studies. I told them how grateful I was that Nathan was doing so well and how amazed I was that he remembered me coming to see him.

Finally I asked, "Nathan, how can you remember that visit? You seemed so dazed, like you really were not connecting with reality. I don't think you even said one word the entire time we were together. Do you remember that?"

He replied, "How could I forget your visit? I don't remember anything you said, but what I do remember is how you helped me not to feel so alone. You helped me not to be so afraid. That got me through the rest of my stay there, when no one else could visit me and I didn't know what was going to happen. I kept being reminded of that feeling of not being alone, and somehow, deep down, I knew that I would be okay."

I would have never thought. I would have never suspected.

And then I confessed, "Nathan, I want you to know that you helped me not to feel so alone either. You helped me not to be so afraid. You see, that visit to you was the first time I had ever visited one of our students in a psychiatric unit. I was very afraid. I didn't know what to expect. But our visit together helped me see that I can make these visits and not feel so afraid. I realized that I'll never be able to predict what to expect when visiting a student in the psychiatric unit, but that is okay. I knew I would be okay."

I wanted more stories to end well, like Nathan's story had. I had comforted too many parents whose children had died by suicide. I had done the funerals. I knew suicide was the second leading cause of death among college students. I knew the majority of these students had some type of mental illness, most commonly depression, which was treatable, even sometimes curable.

Leah had written in her letter that she struggled with depression. I didn't know what else she struggled with, but I knew she struggled with this.

How could I honor her while at the same time not honor her message?

And why did Leah want this letter read at her funeral anyway? What was she really trying to convey? I wrestled with these questions late into the night as I read and reread her letter, trying to discern what words I would share, alongside her own words, at her funeral.

I thought about how when someone dies, the ritual of a funeral or a memorial service allows us to gather to comfort one another, to try to make sense out of death, and to find hope to face the future unafraid. As I thought about these things—feeling comfort, making meaning, and finding hope—I realized Leah's letter spoke to each of these things. Through her letter, she wanted to comfort those she knew and loved. She wanted to help us make some sense out of her death by sharing why she chose to end her life. And she wanted us to know that, for her, her hope for relief and peace did not lie in life but in death.

Leah had written her own eulogy.

The letter was Leah's story, and she wanted her story shared. She knew her viewpoint would go against what many of us believed and held to be true about suicide: that it was *not* the only alternative, the only hope for relief and peace. But as I read and re-read her letter, I began to sense she did not need us to agree with her decision. What she wanted, it seemed, was for us to *understand* her decision, to understand who she was and why she chose to end her life.

Leah had taken the time to write this letter because she did not want us to ignore her or dismiss her. She did not want us to judge her. She wanted us to understand her. She wanted us to understand her need to put an end to her life.

And so, here was the question: Even if we don't agree with someone else's story, could we genuinely acknowledge it? This may have been what Leah was asking those of us at her funeral. Could we let her share her story without judging her or ignoring her or dismissing her? Could we suspend judgment and honor her by letting her story be told, while, at the same time, not owning it for ourselves?

These were the questions I asked those gathered at her funeral. I asked them before her letter was read, and then again after the reading.

Then I addressed their grief. Even if we could acknowledge Leah's story, we were still left with our own stories, our own lives. We may have been comforted that she was no longer suffering, but it didn't change the reality that she was no longer with us. We still needed to grieve for ourselves. We still needed to make sense for ourselves, find meaning for ourselves, and figure out how to move forward with hope—because hope is what gives us the courage to move forward into the future.

It's not about looking for our lives to look the way they did before. It's about being open to the possibility that despite the sadness and loss and broken dreams, there are endless options of how our grief might be transformed into something new. This is hope.

When I first read Leah's letter, I felt like maybe she didn't have the courage to persevere through her suffering. I felt like maybe she gave up and wanted to write the letter to justify why she gave up. But then I realized it wasn't courage she lacked. It was hope that eluded her.

I remembered a time when hope eluded me. It can be different for everyone, but for me there was a fog—sort of like that vapor of grief—that ever so gradually began to weigh me down. It was so subtle in its permeation that I was not even aware I was becoming enveloped by it. I was not even cognizant that I was disoriented, that I could no longer see clearly. That was why it was so easy to deny it. And so it continued to press in on me. And the more it pressed in, the more my hope seeped out—until one morning, I began to wonder why I was still living. It seemed like such a dreadfully heavy burden to continue to carry on my existence. It would be so much easier not to have to make the effort anymore.

It never occurred to me at the time that I might not always feel this way, that perhaps there was another option out there. I couldn't see any alternatives because the scope of my vision had narrowed so considerably.

Depression had cut off my lifeline to hope.

Perhaps this was what had happened with Leah, too. Perhaps depression had squeezed out her hope by restricting her vision.

It can be easy to forget that depression is not only a feeling of sadness; it is also a condition that alters the way we see ourselves, our life, and our future. It is myopic, and, as a result, it misrepresents our worldview.

For me, it was like putting on a pair of prescription glasses that didn't belong to me. Except that I didn't know they weren't mine; I thought they were right for me. As they distorted my vision, the depression deceived me into believing my options were reduced to only what I could see directly in front of my own two hazy eyes.

When this happens, we lose the capacity to imagine how something good or new could come about. We lose the power to be open to the possibility that there are other options. We lose hope. And hope is what we need to fuel the courage to move forward into the future despite our current realities. Hope is what we need to believe our lives can be transformed.

Usually when a person is terminally ill with a physical disease, they are encouraged to get their affairs in order. They may have time to decide how they want to live out the rest of their lives. Hospice may be called in, able to do their remarkable job of facilitating conversations with the dying person and their family about life and death.

Of course, in these cases death is inevitable, and it may seem like all hope is lost. Yet often what happens is that hope shows up in new ways. Regrets might be confessed; burdens might be lifted; new meaning might be made from life's stories; emotional wounds might be healed; spiritual wholeness might occur; a sense of peace might be embraced within and with others. When people gather around a dying person to facilitate the hard work of their coming to terms with their death and the way they lived their life, transformation can happen.[2]

But a person with a mental illness who begins to plan to end their life is not usually surrounded by family or friends or hospice—people who can help them sort out new ways of noticing how hope might show up, how it might be worthwhile to hang around and discover together the possibilities of how their life might be transformed. That doesn't happen because suicide is a decision usually made in isolation. The person doesn't talk about it.

None of us wants to talk about it. Even those of us who have had depression, those of us who at one time considered suicide as the best option for our lives—even we don't want to talk about it. And when we don't want to talk about it, we don't share the

2. For more on the hope and transformation that is possible at the end of life, see Kerry Egan's excellent book *On Living*.

life-saving stories of transformation that have happened in our own lives. We don't talk about how we found the hope to move forward into the future.

I know this because I don't talk about my own story of depression. I don't talk about how I denied something was wrong for so long that the depression began to manifest itself physically, resulting in multiple surgeries. I don't talk about how a family friend finally suggested my physical ailments might stem from mental issues and recommended I see a counselor. I don't talk about how offended I was by that so-called friend; yet how, nonetheless, I grudgingly went to counseling. Just to prove him wrong. I don't talk about how I wouldn't talk about depression with the counselor for months and months, until, beyond weary with the exertion, I finally conceded that perhaps I might have a *touch* of depression and reluctantly agreed to try some medication.

And because I don't talk about any of that, I also don't talk about how the anti-depressants, along with the therapy, actually helped and how, after some time, I began to feel the heaviness lift, like the fog was beginning to oh-so-slowly dissipate. I don't talk about how my physical symptoms began to disappear and how my mental outlook improved. I don't talk about how, from the vantage point of time and treatment and healing, I began to discover possibilities for my life that I could not even fathom when I was in the midst of the pea-soup fog, the great vapor of sadness. I don't talk about how the elusive hope came round and gave me the courage to move forward into the future. I don't talk about how my life was transformed into something new.

I don't talk about that part of my story because I know what people think about those of us who have or have had a mental illness. The stigma is still very much alive and strong. I'm no different than Leah; I don't want to be judged or dismissed or ignored because of my story. I would rather keep it in the closet than run the risk that people think something is wrong with me.

When there is still such a stigma about mental illness, when there is still such judgment about it, when we know people will think we are crazy, why would any of us be vulnerable enough to offer up our stories to others' scrutiny?

The only reason I can imagine we would do this—and it was a reason that had not occurred to me prior to reading Leah's letter—is because our stories of transformation might be just what someone needs to contemplate a possibility other than suicide. It might be just what someone needs to consider sharing their own story of despair.

When we suspend judgment—of ourselves and of others—it opens up a space for stories to be shared and hope to find a way back in. Maybe Leah's letter is a legacy, a gift left behind to encourage us to suspend judgment—in our hearts and in our homes and in our communities—and make a way for hope to transform our stories.

The director of the campus Counseling Center asked if I would come and bless their space as she and the other counselors prepared for a new semester of students, as they prepared anew to listen without judgment to the students' stories. So I went and offered a blessing for them.

> *May all that is sacred,*
> *peace and grace*
> *and goodness and light,*
> *soak into the structures of this place;*
> *the walls that have absorbed the sorrow,*
> *the rooms that have held the grief,*
> *the floors that have allowed the tears to fall upon them,*
> *the air that has carried the scent of despair.*
>
> *May all of this space be redeemed*
> *by all that is sacred;*
> *may the walls and the rooms*

and the floors and the air,
and all that is part of this place
be blessed with peace and grace
and goodness and light.

May it be a sanctuary for all who enter,
that they may find hope
being rekindled in their hearts.

And for those of you
who are keepers of the stories
that have been told here,
who, like the walls and the rooms
and the floors and the air,
have absorbed the sorrow,
and held the grief,
and felt the tears,
and carried the despair;
may each of you be blessed
for being guardians of this sacred space,
for being guardians of our students' stories.

May you be blessed
for your compassion
and your wisdom
and your courage.

May all that is good and gracious
and peaceful and light
refresh your spirit
and renew hope in your heart.

CHAPTER 9

Starbucks 101

Practice of Nurture: Honor Our Spiritual Connection

ONE OF THE CAMPUS ministers was giving me some unsolicited feedback about his perception of my role on campus. He said he didn't think I was religious enough.

I looked at him in surprise. "Not religious enough? Of course I'm religious. I'm a religious professional."

"Yeah, that may be, but you don't *act* religious," was his retort.

I was offended. "What do you mean by that? How do you think someone religious is supposed to act?"

"What I mean is you don't hold religious services on campus, and you don't use religious vocabulary, and you don't even wear a clerical collar at the official events of the college, where you've been asked to give the invocation, where you are in an official capacity as a religious professional."

Well . . . I had to admit that much was true.

But that wasn't all there was to being religious, was it?

It wasn't the first time I had been told I wasn't religious.

I thought about Susan, who initially had thought I was religious but then decided I wasn't. I met her when I went to check on her son, Austin, who was in the hospital with a bad case of the flu that had turned into pneumonia.

I knocked on his open door and stepped inside, looking at the young man in the hospital bed. "Hi, my name is Melynne," I said. "Are you Austin?"

He nodded yes, and I continued, "I'm the chaplain from the college. I wanted to come by and see how you're doing."

Just then, I noticed movement out of the corner of my eye. I turned my head and saw a woman who looked to be about my age sitting in a chair in the shadows of the room.

"Oh, hi," I said. "I didn't realize anyone else was here."

"I'm Austin's mom, Susan," she tersely said as she stood up.

She walked to the end of Austin's bed and planted her feet in a defensive stance right in front of me. I was one second shy of reaching out my hand to shake hers when she crossed her arms over her chest and examined me.

"I'd like to know why you're here visiting my son," she said. "What do you want?"

I was taken aback but not unaccustomed to this kind of welcome. Not everyone gets excited when the chaplain comes to call. And it didn't escape my notice that she had strategically placed herself between her son and me.

I plowed ahead. "Hi, Susan. It's nice to meet you. As I just mentioned, I'm the chaplain at the college, and—"

"That's why I want to know why you're here," she interrupted. "We're not religious, and I don't want a pastor or chaplain or whatever you call yourself coming to visit my son. I don't want him to have any visits from anyone affiliated with the church."

I leaned around Susan and glanced at Austin, who was rolling his eyes behind his mother's back. I knew that look; it was the same one my kids used when they were embarrassed by something I had said or done.

I straightened back up, smiled at Susan, and said, "I understand. And I certainly want to respect the wishes of you and your son. But I'm not here on behalf of a particular church. I'm here on behalf of the college. I serve as the college liaison when a student is hospitalized."

Susan, still in interrogative mode, pursed her lips, tightened her arms across her chest, and asked suspiciously, "What do you mean when you say 'the college liaison'?"

I continued on cheerily. "I'll check in on Austin, and you, periodically, to see how Austin is progressing. And if either of you needs anything from the college or needs to communicate with anyone from there, I can take care of that for you, so you and Austin don't have to worry about it. Also, if you need hotel accommodations, I can help you find a place to stay. And whatever else you might need while you're here. My role is to support Austin in whatever way I can so all his energy can go toward his healing. And my role is also to support you so your energy can go toward supporting Austin."

Susan seemed to mull this over.

She turned and looked back at her son, who offered, "Sounds like a good idea, Mom. You know, I haven't contacted my professors yet. Maybe the chaplain can do that for me."

I stepped around Susan to the end of Austin's bed so I could speak to him directly. "Absolutely. I'll let the Dean of Students Office know. They'll be able to look up your schedule and send out an email to all your instructors. And this way, getting it straight from the dean's office, they'll know it's legit and that you aren't just trying to get out of classes for a few days."

Austin laughed and said, "That's cool. One less thing to worry about it. And what about my RA? Can you let him know, too, so he doesn't think I've gone missing?"

"Sure. Consider it done," I replied as I dug in my purse for a pen and my pad to jot down notes. "If you think of anything else, just let me know." I scrounged in my bag again and brought out two of my business cards and handed one to each of them.

Susan, whose posture had relaxed somewhat, reached out and took the card. She looked down at it and then said, "That actually sounds like a really nice thing the college does for students and their families. I'm sorry if I was rude; it's just that I have issues with the church. I don't want anyone coming in here preaching at my son or trying to convert him, especially in his compromised state."

"I know what you mean," I concurred. "I have a son around Austin's age who is away at school, and as a mother I would feel the same way if he were in the hospital. It's a stressful time for both of you."

Susan took a step closer to me, leaned in, lowered her voice to almost a whisper, and confided, "I was so scared when I got the phone call that he had fallen ill and was admitted here. I was so far away and didn't know what to do. I didn't know anyone down here to call. It's been hard, and I know we're only at the beginning. So, thank you. Thank you for coming. And again, please accept my apologies."

Austin was in the hospital for two weeks with complications from the pneumonia. On one of my later visits, I came to find out more about Susan's relationship with the church. I stopped by at a time when Austin wasn't there, but I found Susan sitting in a chair by the window, reading a book. She invited me in and told me they had taken Austin downstairs to have a lung x-ray done but that she would welcome a visit.

I sat down in the chair opposite her.

"I want to thank you for coming by so often," she said, as she closed her book. "I'm not really sure why, but I think just being able to connect with you has helped me not worry so much about Austin. It has helped me to calm down and be hopeful instead of just thinking anxious thoughts about what might happen. I'm ashamed to think about how I reacted when you first came to visit, thinking you were religious. You're not religious at all."

I tried to cover my surprise. "Well, actually, I *am* religious," I said. "I'm a clergyperson, after all. But a minister working out in the community sometimes looks different from a minister working in a church."

"Yeah, you can say that again. I used to go to church. But not anymore."

"What happened?" I asked.

She took a deep breath and exhaled slowly. "It wasn't any one thing. Maybe it was everything. I don't know. I think what it came down to is that it just seemed that the church, the pastor, the people, whoever, they all seemed to have this prescribed way that we are supposed to think about God and feel about God and respond to God. And you know, it made me feel like I didn't belong there if I couldn't be just like them. It just felt so stilted to me, so stagnant. It was hard to connect with the people, and it was hard to connect with God, too, in a place like that."

Susan paused and looked out the window, then continued. "I began to realize that I felt more connected to God when I wasn't in church than when I was. Whenever I was out biking on the trails around my home, I felt connected with God through the natural beauty around me. This was so much more real to me than sitting in a pew, listening to someone tell me the way I was supposed to feel. So I started looking for more ways to connect with God in nature—like going to a park or just sitting out on my back patio, listening to the birds in the morning. And the more I connected with God in these ways, the less I felt the need for church."

I looked out the window, too, and considered my words. "That makes sense. Sometimes I feel like I connect better with God in nature too. I live near a river and being near that water helps me feel near to God."

Susan nodded, then sighed. "I know people at church probably think I can't possibly have any kind of connection with God if I'm not attending church. But that's not true. I feel more connected to God now than I ever did going to church. I guess you would call me one of those 'spiritual but not religious' people."

She looked at me intently. "And you may say you are religious, but I think you're actually more like me—spiritual but not religious."

I wasn't really sure how she had come to this conclusion. I decided to try and clarify.

"You know, Susan, even though I don't work in a church, I'm still very much connected with the church. I attend church services, and I even sometimes connect with God there. Doesn't that make me religious?"

"No, not really. You don't act religious."

"Tell me more about what you mean by that."

"I don't think it's just going to church that makes someone religious. I don't even think that being ordained necessarily makes someone religious. This whole time you've been visiting Austin and me, you never once told us how we should think about God or how we should feel about God. But we still ended up connecting. It just felt more like a spiritual connection than a religious connection."

I still didn't feel like I was clear on how she was using these two terms, so I pushed further. "What do you see as the difference?"

She responded, "I feel like a religious connection is when someone tells you their beliefs about God, and if you believe the same way, then you might connect religiously. Like how the people at my old church were. But spiritual connection is when you might believe different things about God, but you are able to connect anyway. So I don't think it's just about whether or not you go to church; it's about whether you can recognize that people have their own way of connecting with God. I felt like you and I connected in a way that brought me peace and hope."

My conversation with Susan about spiritual connection reminded me of a conversation I had with Dr. Miller, one of the professors on campus. Dr. Miller and I had first been introduced to one another when we both happened to attend a diversity training seminar for faculty and staff. The instructor was teaching about respect for difference and equitable treatment in the workplace, and at the end of the session, when she asked if there were any comments or questions, Dr. Miller stood up and complained about the prayers being said at the commencement ceremonies.

"As an atheist, I don't think I should have to be subjected to prayers being said at a secular event," he said. "Where is the respect and equity for those of us who don't believe in God?" he asked. "I don't even go to graduation anymore because it's just not right," he finished, and with a weighty sigh sagged back down into his seat.

The auditorium had fallen completely quiet, waiting to see how the instructor would respond. But she was left tongue-tied. She didn't know what to say or do. A couple of people, who knew who I was, ventured a look my way. I raised my eyebrows back at them as if to say *What do you want me to do about it? I'm not in charge of this training.*

But as they continued to stare at me, I realized that perhaps I should say something. Clearing my throat, I slowly rose from my seat and said, "Uh, hi everyone," giving a half-hearted wave of my hand. "I'm the chaplain that says the prayers at the commencement ceremonies so perhaps that might be a question I could address."

The color came back into the instructor's face and she nodded enthusiastically while everyone else turned my way expectantly.

But I had no idea what to say. I didn't make the rules; the administration did. And I didn't think I could just change the rules without checking with them first. So finally, I said, "Perhaps Dr. Miller and I can get together for a conversation about this, about how we might make commencement more equitable for all."

And that was how he came to be sitting in my office ready to discuss religious equity on campus. Apparently not one for small talk, he dove right in.

"I really like the work you've done with the different religious groups on campus," he said, "and how you've advocated for understanding and appreciation of different religious expressions."

I could hear a *but* coming.

"But I don't think you've gone far enough," he added. "I would like to see you also advocating for those of us who are not religious, who don't believe in God. Atheists deserve to be treated with dignity and respect, too, and it's usually the religious people who disrespect us more than those who are not religious."

He was probably right about that.

"I agree with you, Dr. Miller. And I'm embarrassed to say I really haven't given much thought to what it would look like for my office to advocate for atheists. Do you have any ideas for how we might live that out?"

Dr. Miller smiled. "Well, I have several ideas. One of them has to do with what I mentioned at the in-service training, about the graduation ceremony each semester, when you do the invocation and benediction."

I took a deep breath. I knew this would be what he wanted to discuss but I also knew it could be a thicket of brambles to weed through. I reminded myself to stay curious.

I said, "I'm not sure where the tradition of having an opening and closing prayer at graduation came from. Our college is not religiously affiliated, and we never have been, have we?"

I knew Dr. Miller had been at the school a long time and probably knew its history better than I did.

He responded, "No, we've never been religiously affiliated—which, by the way, is one of the reasons I chose to teach at this school. I assumed I would be free from any kind of religious obligation in a non-sectarian institution. But then we began having prayers at the graduation ceremonies. I think it was one of the past presidents who started the tradition. He was religious, and he thought having the prayers in the ceremony was a nice touch."

I thought it was a nice touch, too, invoking the sacred on behalf of the people, asking blessings for the graduates as they began new chapters in their lives. This could be a dilemma.

I proceeded cautiously. "You know, I don't think the current administration would let us take the prayers out," I said. "I'm pretty sure they want them to stay in. But I've tried to offer the prayers in a non-sectarian way, in a way people from all different religious backgrounds could feel comfortable saying 'Amen' or 'Shalom' or 'May it be so.'"

"Yes, and I think you've done a marvelous job with it," he said. "I would not change one thing that you do with the prayers."

"Oh?" I was baffled. I had assumed he would want them removed. "Then what are you suggesting?"

"Well, those of us who are atheist, we don't pray. And there are others who are not people of prayer, either, like some Buddhists and people from some of the other philosophical traditions.

So, to be asked to stand for the invocation and then again for the benediction requires our participation."

"No one is requiring your participation, Dr. Miller."

He held up his hand, "Let me just finish."

I pressed my lips together and nodded for him to go ahead.

He continued, "Of course, we could stay seated, but that would look like we are protesting. I don't want to protest the prayers. For those who are people of prayer, I think they should be able to pray. I don't want to protest that. I just would like for there to be some expression of respect for those who prefer not to participate, out of their own religious or non-religious convictions."

I considered this.

"So, how would you recommend we go about inviting those of you who don't want to participate to abstain?" I asked. Even my question sounded complicated.

Dr. Miller proposed, "I think some kind of statement when you ask people to rise for the prayers could be added. Something like, 'If you would like to join together in a spirit of prayer, please stand as I offer the invocation.' Then that acknowledges there may be some people present who would not choose to do so. It shows respect for both those who are people of prayer and those who are not."

I thought about this and about the school's commitment to religious and non-religious expression on campus. Because we were not religiously affiliated, we did not endorse any specific religion, and we did not endorse religion over non-religion. We encouraged students, staff, and faculty to practice their religious and non-religious beliefs but not to impose their beliefs on others. All religious activity should be voluntary.

In light of that, I could see how asking people to stand for the prayers at graduation could be a conflict of our values. If it was expected for everyone to stand, then it wasn't really voluntary, was it? I had not really thought about it like that before.

If we had been a religiously affiliated school, it would have been different; a religious graduation ceremony would be part of our identity, and it would be disrespectful for those entering into our community not to honor that. But because our identity was not a religious one, we had made a commitment not to impose religious practices onto others. Dr. Miller's suggestion would actually help us to better align ourselves with what we said our values were.

I told him, "I think that is something we could do. I'll talk to the administration. And I appreciate you bringing it to my attention. I'm in agreement with you that everyone, religious or not, should be treated with dignity and respect."

We stood up and shook hands, and as Dr. Miller prepared to leave, I said, "I have to say, you don't fit the stereotype in my mind of an atheist. I don't know any atheists personally, but usually I hear that they are vehemently opposed to religion and religious people."

He chuckled. "And you don't fit the stereotype of a religious person. They are usually vehemently opposed to atheists. But the way I look at it is this: just like you don't need to prove to me that God exists for you to believe in God, I don't need to prove to you that God doesn't exist for me not to believe in God. We can still connect with one another by sharing the values we have in common, like respect and kindness."

And with that last word, we said our goodbyes and he walked out the door. I stood there pondering our conversation as I watched him walk down the hallway.

Dr. Miller might have been atheist, but he was still spiritual, I realized. He embodied the spiritual values of compassion and equity, which arose from that place within him—his spirit—that seeks connection, meaning, and purpose.

Some of us may be deeply devoted to God, and some of us may not even believe there is a God. Some of us may participate in the religious practices of our faith, and others of us may live out our faith in a different way. Some of us may not be people of faith but may still end up reflecting the goodness of God. Whether we seek God inside organized religion or out in nature or not at all, *spiritual* is a common denominator for all of us.

When I was hired as the college chaplain, my job description read, "To nurture the spiritual life of the campus community, with a particular focus on Protestant Christian students." It was presumed by me—and by everyone else—that *spiritual life* was synonymous with *faith life* or *religious life*. To nurture the spiritual life of the campus community was understood to mean that I was to encourage those who were people of faith and to particularly work with those who were from my own religious background.

Once I had begun to contemplate discontinuing the Protestant chapel service I had inherited, I realized my job description needed to be broader. As the first employed chaplain at the college, my role shifted to focus on *all* religious students, not just one subset. So, I learned what it meant to nurture the spiritual life of students from different faith traditions.

Eventually, because of interactions with people like Susan and Dr. Miller, I discovered my job description needed to be broader still, broad enough to encompass non-religious students too. But I wasn't sure I knew what it meant to nurture the spiritual life of students who didn't profess a faith commitment. What does *spiritual* look like when it is not a part of faith or religion?

I thought back to my hospital chaplaincy internship, where we were taught how to evaluate the spiritual health of our patients. That involved looking at questions such as: Were they self-aware? Did they have the capacity to be compassionate with themselves and with others? Did they have meaningful connections with others, with a higher power, with creation, with the universe? Did they feel like they belonged? Did they feel a sense of responsibility to something bigger than themselves? Did they have the ability to make sense out of what was happening in their lives? Could they cultivate hope for themselves? Were they able to discern direction for their lives? These were questions of connection, meaning, and purpose. *Spiritual* referred to that part of us—our spirit—that seeks connection, meaning, and purpose.

What I came to discover was that every one of us has that piece within us; *everyone* has a spirit. For some, nurturing their spirit might include connecting with God through a religious community. For others, it might involve connecting with God without religious practices. And for still others, it may not be about religion or God at all.[1]

Like at Starbucks, for instance.

I first learned that Starbucks was in the spiritual business when I attended a staff workshop on vision and mission. The dean of students, Theresa, wanted to help us understand our mission in broader terms, so she brought up several examples of companies that have expansive mission statements.

"Does anyone know the mission of the Coca-Cola Company?" she asked as she clicked to a PowerPoint slide of a bottle of coke next to a polar bear lounging in the Arctic.

Several of us called out, "To make the best soda!"

"Wrong," she replied. "Think bigger."

The director of Greek life said, "To make the best drinks."

Some of the younger staff giggled, but we all nodded our heads, agreeing with his answer.

"You're thinking too small," was Theresa's response. She goaded us on. "Think bigger. Broader."

But we were stumped. We looked at one another and shrugged our shoulders. No one had an answer.

Theresa sighed, then clicked to the next slide and read, "Coca-Cola's mission: to refresh the world . . . to inspire moments of optimism and happiness . . . to create value and make a difference."[2]

Murmurs of surprise echoed around the room. One of the first-year advisors said, "Wow. Impressive. That mission is so much bigger than putting out a good product."

---

1. For more on defining spirituality, measuring spiritual qualities, and evaluating spiritual development and growth in college students, see Astin et al., *Cultivating the Spirit.*

2. See https://www.coca-colacompany.com/our-company/mission-vision-values.

Theresa clapped her hands and said, "Exactly! That's the way I want you all to think about the missions for your own departments. Think beyond what's in front of you. I'll give you one more example, and then I want you all to brainstorm some ideas."

She clicked on the next slide, which was a photo of the campus Starbucks coffee shop with the familiar green awnings. "What's the mission of Starbucks?" she asked.

Most of us yelled out in unison, "To make the best coffee!"

Theresa was dumbfounded. And exasperated. "Did you all not learn anything from the last example?"

We slouched in our chairs, hangdog looks on our faces.

Impatient with our inability to think big, she clicked to the next slide and read, "The mission of Starbucks: to inspire and nurture the human spirit—one person, one cup, and one neighborhood at a time."[3]

I sat up straighter in my chair. I wasn't sure I accurately heard what I thought I just heard Theresa say. But there it was up on the screen: "To inspire and nurture the human spirit."

I grabbed my iPad from my bag, looked up starbucks.com, and found my way to their company page. Sure enough, there it was: "To inspire and nurture the human spirit."

Who would have thought Starbucks and the Chaplain's Office would have the same mission?

Oblivious now to the goings-on in the room, I continued to read about Starbucks' mission. The page read, "From the beginning, Starbucks set out to be a different kind of company. One that not only celebrated coffee and the rich tradition, but that also brought a feeling of connection."[4]

I recalled some of my interactions at Starbucks and how I had felt a connection with the barista taking my order through something as simple as her looking into my eyes as she asked, "The usual?" If I got someone who hadn't met me yet, they always asked my name. I knew it wasn't just so it made it easier to tell whose drink was whose—after all, most places simply used numbers. It

3. See https://www.starbucks.com/about-us/company-information.
4. See https://www.starbucks.com/about-us/company-information.

was also about them making a connection with me. When they used my name, I felt like I had been seen and valued as a person; I wasn't just a number. Creating connections with others has the capacity to bring meaning and purpose to our lives, and to the lives of others too. This is how Starbucks nurtures our spirit.

Nurturing our spirit can create a sense of peace and balance in our lives. It can help us to be consistent between what we believe and how we behave. And it can cultivate connection, meaning, and purpose in our lives in a way that contributes not only to our own good but to the common good as well.

Honoring our spiritual connection and nurturing spiritual values in one another can lead to an appreciation that we all have the capacity to nurture the common good in one another. We all have the capacity to make the world a better place, to make the vision of shalom—peace on earth—a reality.

A few months after my conversation with Dr. Miller, one of our international students who was just about to finish up his graduate studies died in a car accident on one of our local roads. His mother made the long, somber journey from Korea to our campus to claim and accompany her son's body back home.

Once she arrived, we offered to hold a memorial service for her son. She expressed her gratitude for this through the words of another student who served as a translator because the mother did not speak or understand English. She conveyed through our translator that in their Buddhist tradition, the relative closest to the deceased is to light a candle at the beginning of the funeral.

And so, as the service began, I escorted this grieving mother up the center aisle of our chapel sanctuary to the candle sitting on the altar table. When I handed her the lighter her hands began to shake so fiercely as sobs racked her body that she could not get the candle lit. She looked at me with desperation in her eyes, and I interpreted her look as a plea for help. So, as she held the lighter,

I enveloped her hand in both of mine and held it steady. Finally, slowly, she was able to light the candle.

The physical connection between our hands burned like the candle flame, and when she turned and looked into my eyes again, I knew she felt it too. Some kind of connection touched a place deep within us, beyond words, beyond the touch of skin on skin. It was a place within our spirits where she knew I shared in her grief and I knew she felt my comfort. We stood there, hand in hand, a moment longer, gazing at the glimmer of light in the space between us.

CHAPTER 10

Bidets in the Bathrooms

Practice of Nurture: Recognize the Gifts of Others

THE MUSLIM STUDENTS WANTED bidets in the chapel bathrooms. I didn't know much about bidets, but I did know they had always seemed a bit strange to me. I had never used one. I wasn't even really sure how to go about it. Or why one should. Or would.

Omar and Ahmed, two students from the Middle East, came to my office on behalf of the Muslim Student Association to request that portable bidets (*portable* bidets?) be installed in the bathrooms in our chapel building. They told me bidets were an important part of what it means to be a faithful Muslim; cleanliness is next to holiness, they said, and bidets keep you cleaner. They had literature to substantiate their claim and placed several pamphlets on my desk.

"Cleaner than what?" I asked, as I gingerly picked up one of the pamphlets. I really did not have a clue what they were talking about.

"Cleaner than using toilet paper," Ahmed replied. He went on to explain that when you used toilet paper, you were not always able to wipe adequately, but the water from the bidet would get everything clean.

I gathered we were talking about the best way to wipe after a bowel movement. I could not believe I was having this conversation, especially with two male Muslim students from the Middle East. I studied the young men's earnest faces; they didn't appear to be the least bit uncomfortable. They didn't seem to be aware that we didn't talk about these things in public, at least not in this country, at least not in mixed company.

I resolved not to blush.

Omar and Ahmed went on to tell me how little the bidets cost and how easy they were to install on the existing toilets in our bathrooms.

I could not envision this, so I asked them to show me.

We walked across the hall to the men's restroom. After they made sure it was empty, they called for me to come inside. We crammed into the handicapped stall, and they showed me how a bidet could be attached to the toilet and the tubing connected with the plumbing from the sink (which was why the bidet would need to be installed in the handicapped stall), and then fresh water could run through it when the switch on the bidet was turned on. They assured me that students who didn't want to use the bidet could still use the toilet.

I was trying to think through the logistics of this, and also the theological rationale, but something just didn't make any sense to me. I finally asked them, "So, if you don't want to use toilet paper to wipe, how do you get dry once you have used the bidet? Do you wait for the water to evaporate? Or do you pull your pants back up with your butt still wet?"

I was serious about my question, but they both burst out laughing. Then Omar exclaimed, "Of course not!" He graciously clarified, "We *use* toilet paper, just not to wipe. We use it after we have used the bidet to *pat* the water dry."

Ahhh.

I laughed at my own ignorance and reminded myself—and them—that I had never used a bidet. They both encouraged me to consider trying one out. They said I would never go back to wiping with toilet paper. I thanked them for enlightening me about sanitary toilet habits and told them I would see what I could do about getting bidets installed in both the men's and women's restrooms here in the chapel.

As we left the bathroom, I glanced at myself in the mirror above the sinks, and then stopped when I noticed the purple sweater in my reflection. I looked down at my arms and saw that, indeed, I was wearing my purple sweater.

I had bought the sweater a few months prior, after a shopping trip with my sister-in-law, Stephanie, and my daughter, Meredith. We had gone to T.J.Maxx, and as we combed through the racks of clothes, Stephanie came across a purple cardigan sweater. She asked me, "Do you ever wear purple?"

"Nope. Never. Not my color," I replied.

"Really? I think purple would look good on you. Why don't you try on this sweater?"

I wasn't interested. "I don't wear purple," I responded, and turned back to the racks.

But that wasn't the end of it. When we got to the dressing rooms, Stephanie handed me the purple sweater and again suggested I try it on.

I finally relented.

Once I had it on, I looked at myself in the mirror and thought, *Ugh, this is not my color.* I called out from my dressing room, "I told you! This is not my color!"

I was about to take it off when Stephanie insisted I come out so she could see for herself. When I did, her eyes lit up, as did Meredith's, and they both exclaimed how they loved the color purple on me.

I looked at them, looked at myself in the mirror, looked back at them, then looked again at myself. I was trying to see what they saw, but as much as I scrutinized myself, I couldn't recognize it. I didn't like the color purple on me. Much to their protests, I didn't buy the sweater.

Weeks later, though, I was still thinking about that sweater. Not so much about the sweater itself, but about the color purple. I couldn't remember wearing, or even trying on, the color purple, so I was not sure how my bias against wearing that color came to be. I went out the next day and bought myself the purple sweater. I wanted to live with my bias out in the open, right on my arms. I wanted this purple sweater to show me other biases I might have that I was not even aware of yet.

And that day in the bathroom with the Muslim students, it did just that.

Once the bidets were put in, word got out and the Muslim students, the majority of whom were from other countries, came to the chapel in droves to have their morning constitution. This might sound humorous, but I didn't laugh or even chuckle when I would see a Muslim student come in and go straight to the restroom. Rather, I felt gratitude.

Previously, I had sought to welcome these students in various ways, hoping to help them feel at home on the campus and in the religious space of the chapel building, but nothing I had done compared to the welcome they felt once the bidets showed up. It was a gift the two Muslim students had provided for their community on campus. As the students came in to use the restroom each morning, I could tell they felt a little more at home in this foreign country.

I was grateful Omar and Ahmed showed up in my office that day, and I was grateful that, despite my unrecognized bias, I didn't brush off their request. I was grateful I followed them into the bathroom, where I unwittingly learned a lesson in the art of hospitality. In that space between us, Omar and Ahmed became a gift to me as I discovered the sacred in our midst. Who would have ever imagined a bathroom stall could be a sacred space?

࿒

In Richard Rohr's book *The Divine Dance*, he describes the sacred "spaces in between" the three members of the Christian Triune God as "diffused, intuitive, mysterious, and wonderful unconscious in-between."[1] When I read this recently, I was intrigued with this depiction of the spaces in between. I looked up the words *diffuse, intuition, mystery,* and *unconscious* on dictionary.com: "To intermingle." "Direct perception of truth . . . independent of any reasoning process." "Anything that remains unexplained or unknown." "Not perceived at the level of awareness; occurring below the level of conscious thought."

It made me wonder: Might this be what had happened that day with Omar and Ahmed, when we stuffed ourselves inside a bathroom stall so they could show me how a portable bidet worked? Something happened in that space between us. Something happened on a level below the level of conscious thought. I can't explain it, at least not logically or rationally. I can't define it. The most I can do is describe the effects of it.

Something in the space between us touched my spirit. I would say it was a spiritual encounter for me. I would even call it a sacred encounter. Something happened in that space between us that seemed to be bigger than the space itself and larger than my capacity to make sense of it on the face of it. It left me in awe.

I would even go as far as to say that what happened in that space was, for me, a Eucharistic encounter.

Eucharist, a Greek word meaning "thanksgiving," is another name for the sacrament of Holy Communion, a Christian ritual. A sacrament is something that reveals the spiritual through physical, material, tangible ways. In the church, Eucharist is celebrated with bread and wine, both physical elements that are used as a means to reveal God's presence to us.

I remember how I explained it to Toii, an exchange student from Norway who came to live with our family for a semester back when my daughter, April, was still in high school. Toii was

1. Rohr, *Divine Dance*, 94.

unfamiliar with Christian traditions and rituals. She had been raised as a Humanist and had not been exposed to Christian beliefs or practices in her family home or in her native country. So the first Sunday she asked to go to church with us, she had a lot of questions, especially about Eucharist.

I shared with her that the bread is a symbol of Christ's body and the cup is a symbol of Christ's blood. Immediately she wanted to know why we would want to eat Christ's body and drink Christ's blood. I told her we don't believe the bread and the cup are *literally* Christ's body and blood. I asked her to think about bread in our everyday lives. It is a source of nourishment; it is what keeps us alive at a very basic level. I said the same is true of blood, that if we think of donating blood to someone, then we are giving them the gift of life, as blood is what sustains life.

A lot of people in the church tend to think Eucharist has to do with death because it was at the Last Supper, before Christ's death, that he took bread and wine and told the disciples, "Do this in remembrance of me." But Eucharist actually has a lot more to do with life than death. Through it, we encounter the living Spirit of Christ in our midst. We are reminded God does not sit on a throne up in the sky somewhere but rather is present and active right here on earth. Eucharist bears witness to, and makes visible, God's presence with us.

I shared with Toii that in receiving Eucharist, we believe the Spirit of God nourishes us and sustains us—not physically, the way bread nourishes and blood sustains our bodies, but spiritually. In the act of eating a piece of bread dipped in a splash of wine, we have the opportunity to experience the unconditional acceptance of God. This is what the church calls grace.

If I were to have a conversation with Toii today about Eucharist, I would want to elaborate on my explanation. I would tell her Eucharist is not something only reserved for church on Sunday or even limited to bread and wine. Eucharist can happen anywhere at any time with any kind of elements. An experience of Eucharist doesn't depend on the church alone or the clergy alone. It doesn't even depend on Christians alone. God can come to any of us anywhere we are and use any kind of ordinary everyday object—like bread or wine or water or mud, or even a bidet—as a way to nourish and sustain us.

The experience of Eucharist might be a sense of peace, or hope, or comfort, or conviction. It might be a sense of well-being, or a sense of welcome, a sense that we can be at home in the world, at home in our own skin, that we are safe, that we are enough. It might be a sense that we are not alone, that we are connected to someone else or something bigger than ourselves. Eucharist helps us recognize the spiritual in the midst of the material, concrete realities of life.

Material, concrete objects can create opportunities to experience sacred space with one another. It's similar to the way we might invite friends over for dinner. The food is not the main event, but it offers a way for us to open up a space to connect with one another on a deeper level, which then becomes the main event.

In the church, Eucharist is planned, and the specific elements of bread and wine are used. The people anticipate participating in this ritual as a means of encountering God's presence and receiving God's grace. Outside of the church, however, we often have no idea what might end up being a channel of God's grace, or a means of connecting with one other on a deeper level, or a way of entering into a space that may eventually be described as sacred.

When I first began working as the college chaplain, I wanted my work to be a Eucharistic ministry, one in which I would look for and bear witness to God's presence showing up in ordinary places and in everyday ways. I wanted to facilitate for others the reception of God's grace. In essence, I anticipated that I would offer Eucharist to others. What I had not anticipated, however, was that others would offer the gift of Eucharist to me; that is, they would somehow—knowingly or unknowingly—facilitate for me the reception of God's grace. I realize now, though, that this is what happened, time and time again.

Who would have ever thought bidets could be Eucharistic? The whole idea of a bidet still seems so strange to me. For the Muslim students, though, and a lot of other students from countries where it is common, a bidet is something they use every single day. They wouldn't think twice about it, the way I don't think twice about my toilet habits.

It wasn't until I went to visit my dear friend in Japan recently that I discovered the Japanese people do not have the same toilet customs as I have in the United States. Before my trip, it had never occurred to me that my toilet customs were called *Western*, and that the Japanese accommodate many of the Westerners who visit their country by providing Western toilets, alongside traditional Japanese toilets, in the restrooms in many of the stores and train stations and even in some of the temples. Something as seemingly mundane as a Western toilet turned out to be, for me, a comfort that helped me to feel more welcomed, more at home in a foreign country.

My experience there reminded me of the bidets back at the chapel and how they helped the students feel a little more comfortable, a little more welcomed, a little more at home in a strange place. This gives me a glimpse of how I imagine God welcomes us, the way Omar and Ahmed welcomed me, into the sacred space between us.

CHAPTER 11

The Moon is Always Full

Practice of Nurture: Bless One Another

THE IMAM WAS MISSING from his table. I found him over at the Catholic table, introducing himself to the priest. The Catholic table was next to the Jewish table, where several people were helping themselves to donuts the rabbi had brought in for everyone.

We were in the middle of the university's Student Center at lunchtime. I had organized an event for students to connect with leaders from our local faith communities. We had set up tables for each of the faith leaders who came, but none of them were where they were supposed to be.

The rabbi had abandoned his donuts and was over visiting with the Presbyterian youth director. The Methodist pastor was engaged in conversation with the Buddhist sensei. The priest from the Episcopal Church was hanging out with the college pastor from the Pentecostal church.

Then I saw Lucia, the wife of the pastor from the Spanish-speaking Southern Baptist church, coming toward me.

Uh oh.

Even though we belonged to the same religion, our beliefs about so many things, from salvation to women to how we read the Bible, were vastly different. Lucia believed heaven was a place you went after you died; I believed it was a place we created here on earth. She believed women should be under the authority of men in the church; I believed women and men had equal gifts and should use them accordingly. She took the words of the Bible literally; I interpreted them contextually. What could we talk about that wouldn't put us at odds with one another?

She sat down next to me, and as we began to chat, she apologized that her English was not very good. She explained she and her husband were born and raised in Mexico and had lived there until a few years ago, when they joined their adult daughter, Isabel, and her husband here in the States.

Intrigued, I asked how her daughter came to be in the United States. Lucia told me that Isabel came here to study about ten years ago, fell in love with an American man, eventually married him, and settled in this country. My new friend confided to me how very difficult that time was for her as she contemplated Isabel living the rest of her life in a foreign country, away from her family.

This brought up in me worries I had about my own daughter, April, who was studying abroad in Buenos Aires for a semester of her junior year of college. What if she fell in love and settled down in Argentina, a hemisphere away from me?

I had not wanted April to go to Argentina. I had told her she had enough cultural experience. She had been an exchange student to Austria her junior year of high school, only sixteen years old when she left me that first time, and I had to go see a counselor to help me process my grief. At the end of her sophomore year in college, she went with a group to Ghana for a month. She knew what it meant not to be ethnocentric. She had learned all the things we send students abroad to learn. She didn't need to do it again. I fought her tooth and nail on it, coming up with one good reason after another why she didn't need to study abroad in Argentina.

But then her father stepped in and named all the reasons it would be a good experience for her. Of course he thought she should go; after all, he was the adventurous type. He just wanted to live vicariously through her, I told him. And he wholeheartedly agreed, like there was nothing wrong with that.

This made me stop and wonder if my reasons for not wanting her to go had less to do with her and more to do with me. I began to think through my resistance. What was underneath it all?

Hidden away, squeezed up in a very tight corner of my heart, was a teeny, tiny kernel of a fear that if April went to Argentina, she would fall in love with the country (I had not yet considered the idea of her falling in love with a man) and want to live there permanently after she finished college.

I knew I couldn't let my silly little fear keep her from going. Besides, realistically, what were the odds she would want to live out her life there? So I relented, and April began to make her plans.

Two months into April's four-month semester down there, I sat and listened as Lucia shared her story. And I confessed to her my unspoken fear.

She patted my arm in understanding. I knew she knew it was not a "silly little fear." She had lived with that fear blowing up into reality, but she had also found a way to creatively embrace it.

As her hand connected with my arm, I felt her giving me something, a blessing of sorts. It was intangible but so real, I felt like I could reach out and touch it. In that space we shared, she was no longer just the pastor's wife and I was no longer only the chaplain. We were also mothers together, one of whom had lived through her fear and not only survived but thrived, and could bear witness to the other that, if need be, she could do it too.

A little more than a year later, April was back from her study abroad semester-that-turned-into-her-entire-junior-year in Buenos Aires. Halfway through her senior year of college back here in the States, she was home for her winter break.

On the morning of Christmas Eve, she announced she would return to her college town in Virginia the day after Christmas. I was heartbroken; it felt as though she had only just arrived. She had told me she planned to be home for two weeks; now she would be gone in half that time.

She claimed she wanted to get back to her job at the town's coffee shop so she could earn money for her return trip to Argentina after her college graduation in the spring. This was what she said, but it was not what I heard. What I heard was that she didn't want to be with us, her family, at Christmastime.

This stirred up memories of when I was her age, when I was in college and went to spend the holidays with my fiancé's family instead of my own. It turned out to be the best Christmas present of all, not having to go home to all the dysfunctional messiness that was usually magnified this time of year. I was afraid April felt the same way about us that I had felt about my family of origin, that all she wanted was to get away from us. *Were we dysfunctional? Were we a mess?*

I admitted my fears to her, and she tried to reassure me it simply wasn't true. She said she loved being home with us but wanted to get back to her job at the coffee shop. It was something I couldn't understand as thoughts of my younger self flooded my rational brain. I was despondent the entire day but hid my sadness and fear beneath a cloak of self-righteous anger toward April.

And I kept wondering, *What happened to my little girl who didn't want me to leave her at bedtime? Where was that precious and precocious child who could charm me into staying with her as we read and reread her favorite storybook?* Every night we finished the book with the same ritual of declaring our love for one another. "I love you up to the moon, Mommy," April would say, and my response would always be, "And I love you up to the moon and back."

How could someone who had been such a mama's girl be the same person who, at only sixteen, spent a year in Austria? And then, as a college junior, spent a year in Argentina? And now she was determined to go back there to live. *Why did she always want to leave me?*

At the Christmas Eve service that night, I couldn't bring myself to join in on the lovely carols we sang or the special Scripture passages we read. After we returned home, I was unable to celebrate with the others as we shared delicious desserts and toasted with champagne. I wanted to be filled with peace and hope and joy, but those elusive Christmas sentiments were well beyond my reach as the melancholy enveloped me.

The next morning I went through the motions of making coffee and tea and tried to fix a smile on my face as my grown children found their stockings and discovered the gifts I had stuffed inside. As I watched from a distance, April unwrapped two beautifully crocheted luggage tags.

I had forgotten I bought those for her.

She held them in her cupped hands and then glanced my way, a mesmerized hint of a smile on her face. I couldn't say for sure, but that look on her face made me worry she might consider the luggage tags to be my blessing on her never-ending travels.

I thought back to when I first saw them. They had caught my eye because they looked like April. They were creative and vibrant, the colors of her spirit. But that wasn't the only reason I had bought them for her. It was also because I knew—deep down inside me, I knew—that discovering the world was the way April discovered herself. This was who she was.

I had forgotten this yesterday, when my own history and my own needs stood in the way.

Whether or not I wanted to acknowledge it out loud, I knew the luggage tags were my blessing on April's perpetual leave-taking. I knew they symbolized my maternal longing for her to live into all of who she was, even if it drew her away from me. A snapshot of Lucia patting my arm skimmed across the horizon of my thoughts.

Something softened in me then, and it caused my anger to lose some of its edge, my sadness to lose some of its focus.

After the kids finished with their stockings, they began to pass out their gifts for my husband and me. April came over and gave me a handwritten note and a photo of a painting she said she was having done for me. It was a night scene of the ranch where she had worked while studying in Argentina, with a full moon shining down upon the land.

Her note read, "Dear Mama, I think now more than ever this painting is appropriate. I want it to symbolize that we are always together in spirit, despite our physical location. It has and will continue to comfort me knowing that wherever we are, we are both looking at the same moon. I love you to the moon and back. Love, April."

As I tearfully read the note, I began to hear April's voice, to really hear what she had tried to say to me the previous day. April had blessed me with something I could not demand or declare for myself: the gift of her continual love and devotion, even while she ventured off into her own dreams. The two were not mutually exclusive, I discovered.

And with the luggage tags, I had unknowingly given her my blessing, something I never imagined I would be able to do. I thought back to my conversation with Lucia and how I had presumed we had nothing to offer one another. Yet she had blessed me with her presence and her words in such a way that I was then able to receive April's blessing.

The words from one of Jan Richardson's meditations in *Night Visions* speaks to me about this. Reflecting on a poem written by Barbara Kingsolver, titled "Remember the Moon Survives," Jan muses about "the constant wholeness of the moon" in the midst of "the waxing and waning shadow."[1] The moon is never *not* whole. In other words, there is always a full moon. We just don't see it in all its fullness all the time because of the shadow.

It was my own shadow that hindered me from seeing the fullness of April. And it was the shadow I had cast upon Lucia that at first obscured my view of her fullness. But then, somehow a blessing had the power to shift the shadows so I could more clearly see the fullness of each of them.

John O'Donohue, in his book *To Bless the Space Between Us*, captures the power of blessing. He says, "When a blessing is invoked, it changes the atmosphere. . . . In the light and reverence of blessing, a person or situation becomes illuminated in a completely new way."[2]

Sometimes blessings are intentional; other times they come as complete surprises. What may have been a simple interaction,

1. Richardson, *Night Visions*, 30.
2. O'Donohue, *Bless the Space*, xv.

nothing more than a fleeting encounter, takes on the possibility for blessing when we choose to enter into the common spaces between us and experience the potential to recognize, honor, and nurture the good in one another.

Sometimes it means acknowledging our fears and making room for others by creating a safe space. Sometimes it means remembering we are all human beings, and spiritual beings too. Sometimes it is about paying attention to the worthiness of our own inner voice. Other times it is about suspending judgment and showing kindness, both with others and with ourselves. It is about recognizing the gifts others have to offer, especially when we are inclined to think we are the ones bringing the gifts.

When we do this, then often we are surprised to discover that the shadows have shifted. Maybe we find we have emerged from our own shadow, or perhaps we have laid down the shadow we prescribed to the other. What we know for sure is that the atmosphere has somehow changed and a person or situation is "illuminated in a completely new way." We are able to see and hear and value one another in all our fullness. We become a blessing to one another.

Beyond the shadow the moon is always full.

Bibliography

Astin, Alexander W., et al. *Cultivating the Spirit: How College Can Enhance Students' Inner Lives.* San Francisco: Jossey-Bass, 2011.

The Book of Discipline of the United Methodist Church. Nashville: United Methodist Publishing, 2008.

Brown, Brené. *The Gifts of Imperfection: Let Go of Who You Think You're Supposed to Be and Embrace Who You Are.* Center City, MN: Hazelden, 2010.

Egan, Kerry. *On Living.* New York: Riverhead, 2016.

"Jacinda Ardern on the Christchurch Shooting: 'One of New Zealand's Darkest Days.'" *The Guardian*, March 15, 2019. https://www.theguardian.com/world/2019/mar/15/one-of-new-zealands-darkest-days-jacinda-ardern-responds-to-christchurch-shooting.

Newell, J. Philip. *Celtic Benediction: Morning and Night Prayer.* Grand Rapids, MI: Eerdmans, 2000.

O'Donohue, John. *To Bless the Space Between Us: A Book of Blessings.* New York: Doubleday, 2008.

Richardson, Jan L. *Night Visions: Searching the Shadows of Advent and Christmas.* Cleveland: United Church Press, 1998.

Rohr, Richard. *The Divine Dance: The Trinity and Your Transformation.* New Kensington, PA: Whitaker, 2016.

Wiederkehr, Macrina. *The Song of the Seed: A Monastic Way of Tending the Soul.* New York: HarperOne, 1995.